'As I Said to Denis ...'

'As I Said to Denis ...'

*The Margaret Thatcher
Book of Quotations*

IAIN DALE

Robson Books

First published in Great Britain in 1997 by Robson Books Ltd, Bolsover House, 5–6 Clipstone Street, London W1P 8LE

Copyright © 1997 Iain Dale

The right of Iain Dale to be identified as author of this work has been asserted by him in accordance with the Copyright, Designs and Patents Act 1988

British Library Cataloguing in Publication Data
A catalogue record for this title is available from the British Library

ISBN 1 86105 98 4

Illustrations by John Jensen

Photoset in Palatino in North Wales by Derek Doyle & Associates, Mold, Flintshire. Printed in Great Britain by a Butler & Tanner Ltd, London and Frome.

This book is dedicated to the memory of
Constance Henrietta Dale
1894–1979

Contents

Foreword

It was a cold evening in February. The boy was only twelve years old, yet he knew that something historic had just happened. He tip-toed up the stairs to the bedroom, where his eighty year old grandmother lay in bed, suffering from flu. Having gauged that she was indeed awake, he approached the bed.

The woman who lay there was a formidable personality in her own right. She dominated her family in a matriarchal style, reminiscent of the woman who that day had won the leadership of the Conservative Party.

'She's won,' he said. Silence. 'No, really, she's won,' he protested. Slowly, a tear ran down her face. 'It's not possible,' she murmured. 'It's just not possible.'

That boy was me. Even at such a young age I was interested in politics. I wasn't a Conservative. Only six months earlier, I remember walking into my parents' bedroom with my own thoughts on who should win the general election. I read it to my parents, who quite obviously had a good night's sleep higher on their priority list. 'All the Conservatives ever did was take us into Europe,' I exclaimed. 'The Liberals have no chance of winning.' I said, with a remarkable degree of accuracy. 'So, give Labour a chance,' I advised. 'Don't be so stupid,' said my father. 'Go back to bed.'

My early teenage years were spent supporting David Steel's Liberals. My parents had both voted Liberal in 1974, more as a protest against Edward Heath than anything, but my mother said she would not be able to vote for them again after Jeremy Thorpe had disgraced himself.

Like most of my schoolfriends and teachers I found it easy to poke fun at Mrs Thatcher. It was certainly not fashionable to be a Conservative in the mid 1970s. But one day in October 1978 I heard her speech to the Tory Party Conference. I remember thinking at the end of it that I agreed with virtually everything she said. I got hold of a few policy documents and at the age of 16 I joined the local Conservative Party.

I stood in a mock election at my comprehensive school in the 1979 election as the Conservative Candidate and achieved a 27 per cent majority. In 1982 I formed my University Conservative Association and three years later went to work at the Commons as a researcher to two Conservative MPs. I was a staunch Thatcherite – still am, for that matter. The lady inspired and maintained my interest in politics. I think that can be said for many of my generation. She inspired admiration and hate in equal quantities. Rarely has a British politician ever been so loved and reviled at the same time. Few have been satirised to the degree she was.

But she had her failings too, something even her greatest admirers will readily admit. She was not a particularly good judge of character and made some appalling ministerial appointments, which in the end contributed greatly to her downfall. She was not a good listener, something many a world leader will testify to. But having said that, she loved a good argument. It is said that John Major first came to her notice when he stood up to her and argued his case.

Her achievements outweigh any of her failings. She restored this country's faith in itself, rescued our industry from the shackles of trade union domination and cured the economy of inflation. She fought for freedom and challenged dictators. She played a pivotal role in bringing about the end of Communism, standing firm by the side of President Reagan. She was the first to see that Mikhail Gorbachev was a different kind of Soviet leader. For all this she will be remembered as a dominant force in the final quarter of the twentieth century. Was she one of our great Prime Ministers, joining the ranks of Lloyd George, Churchill, Gladstone, Disraeli and Attlee? History will be the judge.

This book is meant to give the reader both an insight into the character of Margaret Thatcher and her political views and an historical record of the Thatcher years in her own words, and the words of those who were there with her. No collection of quotes can ever be all-encompassing, and this one certainly does not pretend to be. What it does, is show how her personality developed from childhood into the powerful, self-confident politician who achieved the highest office in the land. It includes quotes from her opponents as well as her allies. As the editor, I make no secret of my admiration for Margaret Thatcher and her achievements, but this book is not a hagiography of quotations. It is, instead, an accessible record of the Thatcher years of power.

I would like to thank friends and colleagues who have given frank and helpful advice during the preparation of this book and been of great support to me. They include Audrey Barker, Wendy and Chris Bond, Steve Bramall, Peter and Juliet Clarke, Julia Clarke, Alex Collinson, Peter

Cropper, my parents, Jane and Garry Dale, Sheena Dale, Tracey Dale, Eleanor Daniels, Gabriella and Felix Dasser-Fuchs, Claire Dexter, Daniel Forrester, David and Rosemary Griggs, Michael Fuerst, Helen Houseman, Susan Kerry-Bedell, Stephen Laino, Marjorie Lloyd, Sylvester Michaels, Mark Milosch, Denis and Marion Nicholls, John Parry, Tim Quint, John Simmons, Enid Simmons, Anne Rochford and Deborah Slattery. In addition, I would like to thank the staff of Westminster Reference Library for their kindness and help.

I am grateful to Sir Bernard Ingham for allowing me to reproduce the *Yes, Prime Minister* sketch. Parliamentary copyright material from *Hansard* is reproduced with the permission of Her Majesty's Stationery Office on behalf of Parliament.

I have listed many of the sources for this book in a bibliography at the end as they are too numerous to mention here. Where possible I have provided the original source for the individual quotes, although this has not always been possible. I have also added a contextual explanation where I thought it necessary. Any errors are mine alone.

Finally, I would like to thank Lady Thatcher herself – it can never be more true to say that this book would never have been possible without her.

Iain Dale
January 1997

Early Years

I wasn't lucky – I deserved it.
Receiving a prize for poetry, aged 9

★

I owe a great deal to the church for everything in which I believe. I am very glad that I was brought up strictly ... I was a very serious child ... There was not a lot of fun and sparkle in my life.
Daily Telegraph, *June 1980*

★

I was brought up by a Victorian grandmother. We were taught to work jolly hard. We were taught to prove yourself; we were taught self reliance; we were taught to live within our income. You were taught that cleanliness is next to godliness. You were taught self respect. You were taught always to give a hand to your neighbour. You

1

were taught tremendous pride in your country. All of these things are Victorian values. They are also perennial values. You don't hear so much about these things these days, but they were good values and they led to tremendous improvements in the standard of living.
LBC Radio, April 1983

★

She was a perfectly good second class chemist. None of us ever thought that she would go very far. One could always rely on her to produce a sensible, well-read essay and yet there was something that some people had that she hadn't quite got. I don't believe she had a particularly profound interest in chemistry.
Dorothy Hodgkin, Margaret Thatcher's tutor at Oxford

★

I went to Oxford University, but I've never let that hold me back.
Conservative Party Conference, 13 October 1989

★

This woman is headstrong, obstinate and dangerously self-opinionated.
Report on Margaret Roberts by the ICI Personnel Department, rejecting her job application, 1948

★

When hecklers stand up ... I get a mental jump for joy. It gives me something to get my teeth into – and the audiences love it.
Daily Graphic, *1951*

★

For some time now I have been fleeing the temptation to return to active politics. I had intended, when I was called to the Bar, to concentrate entirely on legal work but a little experience at the Revenue Bar, and in company matters, far from turning my attention from politics, has served to draw my attention more closely to the body which is responsible for the legislation about which I have come to hold strong views.

Letter to Donald Kaberry, Vice Chairman of the Conservative Party, written in February 1956. Path to Power, *1995*

★

I suppose I was about 20, and a crowd of us had been to a village hop and came back to make midnight cups of coffee. I was in the kitchen helping to dish up and having a fierce argument with one of the boys in the crowd when someone else interrupted to say: 'Of course Margaret, you will go into politics won't you?' I stopped dead. Suddenly it was crystallized for me. I knew.

Daily Express, *April 1961*

★

I loved my mother dearly, but after I was 15 we had nothing more to say to each other. It wasn't her fault. She was weighed down by the home, always being in the home.

Daily Express, *April 1961*

★

One of my favourite quotations is: 'That which thy father bequeathed thee, earn it anew, if thou wouldst possess it'.

It is expensive to be in politics. One has to be mobile, one has to be well groomed, and one has to entertain.
Guardian, *March 1962*

★

We must recognize certain groups of people who need help, but the rest of us must take responsibility for ourselves, and we must stop being such a subsidized-minded society.
Scottish Conservative Party Conference, May 1969

★

This business of the working class is on its way out I think. After all, aren't I working class? I work jolly hard, I can tell you.
London Evening News, *October 1969*

★

Comprehensive schools will have gone out in 10 or 15 years' time.
1970

★

I've no idea why people keep attacking me. I don't deserve it at all.
Sunday Express, *16 January 1972*

★

I'm not hard, I'm frightfully soft – but I will not be hounded.
Daily Mail, *1972*

★

Please don't use the word tough. People might get the impression that I don't care. And I do care very deeply. Resilient, I think.
August 1973

★

I enjoyed my early Ministerial career: it was an absorbing education both in the ways of Whitehall and in the technicalities of pensions policy. But I could not help noticing a curious discrepancy in the behaviour of my colleagues. What they said and what they did seemed to exist in two separate compartments. It was not that they conspicuously deceived anyone; they were in fact conspicuously honourable. But the language of free enterprise, anti-socialism and the national interest sprang readily to their lips, while they conducted government business on very different assumptions about the role of the State at home and of the nation-state abroad.
Downing Street Years, 1993

★

I don't want to be leader of the Party – I'm happy to be in the top dozen.
1974

★

We failed the people.
On the Heath Government, Daily Telegraph, *February 1974*

★

It was then that the iron entered my soul.
On the Heath Government

★

We went back on a very similar manifesto to things I believe in. The difference is that after eighteen months to two years he did the biggest U-turn on policy of all time and started to go the wrong way. In the end, that cost us the next election.
On the Heath Government, 18 June 1990

★

The charm of Britain has always been the ease with which one can move into the middle class.
London Evening Standard, *October 1974*

★

Look Keith, if you're not going to stand, I will.
To Sir Keith Joseph after he decided not to stand against Edward Heath for the Party leadership

★

Forget that I'm a woman. Forget the accusations that I am a right winger demanding privilege – I had precious little privilege in my early years.
February 1975

★

I've got my teeth into him, and I'm not going to let go.
On Edward Heath during the leadership contest, February 1975

★

Now we have lots of work to do.
To Norman St John Stevas, who broke the news to her that she had won the first round of the leadership contest, February 1975

★

To me it is like a dream that the next name in the list after Harold Macmillan, Sir Alec Douglas-Home and Edward Heath is Margaret Thatcher.
February 1975

★

I always cheer up immensely if an attack is particularly wounding because I think, well, if they attack me personally it means they have not a single political argument left.

★

The better I do, the more is expected of me. I am ready for that. I think I have the strength to do anything that I feel has to be done.
Daily Telegraph, *September 1975*

On the Road to
Thatcherism

You cannot bring about prosperity by discouraging thrift
You cannot strengthen the weak by weakening the strong
You cannot help the wage earner by pulling down the
wage payer
You cannot further the brotherhood by encouraging class
hatred
You cannot help the poor by destroying the rich
You cannot establish sound security on borrowed money
You cannot keep out of trouble by spending more than
you earn
You cannot build character and courage by taking away
man's initiative and independence
You cannot help men permanently by doing for them
what they could and should do for themselves
Abraham Lincoln, kept by Mrs Thatcher in her handbag

★

We should back the workers, not the shirkers.
February 1974

★

We must have an ideology. The other side have got an ideology they can test their policies against. We must have one as well.
1975

★

Let our children grow tall, and some grow taller than others.
Speech in the United States, 1975

★

We must build a society in which each citizen can develop his full potential, both for his benefit and for the community as a whole.
1975

★

The next Conservative government will look forward to discussion and consultation with the trade union movement about the policies that are now needed to save our country.
Conservative Party Conference, Brighton, October 1976

★

If your only opportunity is to be equal then it is not opportunity.
28 November 1976

★

Britain is no longer in the politics of the pendulum, but of the ratchet.
1977

★

We want a society in which we are free to make choices, to make mistakes, to be generous and compassionate. That is what we mean by a moral society – not a society in which the State is responsible for everything, and no one is responsible for the State.
At Zurich University, 14 March 1977

★

Sometimes I've heard it said that Conservatives have been associated with unemployment. That's absolutely wrong. We'd have been drummed out of office if we'd had this level of unemployment.
Party Political Broadcast, May 1977, when unemployment was 1.3 million

★

If the unions hold the whip hand, upon whose back does the lash fall?
25 September 1977

★

Let me tell you a little about my extremism. I am extremely careful never to be extreme. I am extremely aware of the dangerous duplicity of Socialism, and extremely determined to turn back the tide before it destroys everything we hold dear. I am extremely

disinclined to be deceived by the mask of moderation that Labour adopts whenever an election is in the offing, a mask now being worn by all those who would 'keep the red flag flying here'.
Conservative Party Conference, 14 October 1977

★

We do not believe that if you cut back what government does you diminish its authority. On the contrary, a government that did less, and therefore did better, would strengthen its authority.
Conservative Party Conference, 14 October 1977

★

The counterpart of the withdrawal of government from interference in prices and profits in the private sector which both we and you want to see, is inevitably the withdrawal of government from interference in wage bargaining. There can be no selective return to personal responsibility.
Speech to Scottish industrialists, January 1978

★

There are still people in my party who believe in consensus politics. I regard them as quislings, as traitors ... I mean it.
1978

★

We must learn again to be one nation, or one day we shall be no nation.
1978

★

Today it seems as if people are made to feel guilty about being well off. But Christ did not condemn riches as such, only the way in which they were used and those who put their trust in them.
March 1978

★

This country belongs to the courageous, not the timid.
The Times, *September 1978*

★

I think people are really rather afraid that this country might be rather swamped by people with a different culture and, you know, the British character has done so much for democracy and law, and done so much throughout the world, that if there is any fear that it might be swamped, people are going to be really rather hostile to those coming in.
Granada TV, *January 1978*

★

I have never filled in a pools coupon, so I have never been a winner. But I am going to have a shot from now on.
Following victory in the vote of no confidence in the Callaghan government, 25 March 1979

★

Let us make this country safe to work in. Let us make this country safe to walk in. Let us make it a country safe to grow up in. Let us make it a country safe to grow old in.
In a Party Political Broadcast, 30 April 1979

★

I must warn you, that although our Party is going to win overall, I could lose Finchley.

To her family on the eve of the election in May 1979. She won, almost doubling her majority.

★

Unless we change our ways and our direction, our greatness as a nation will soon be a footnote in the history books, a distant memory of an offshore island, lost in the mist of time like Camelot, remembered kindly for its noble past.

2 May 1979

★

The mission of this government is much more than the promotion of economic progress. It is to renew the spirit and solidarity of the nation.

6 June 1979

★

If a woman like Eva Peron with no ideals can get that far, think how far I can go with all the ideals I have.'

Sunday Times, *1980*

★

Iron entered my soul. You need a touch of steel. Otherwise you become like Indiarubber.

BBC Radio, *March 1980*

★

My politics are based … on things I and millions like me were brought up with. An honest day's work for an honest day's pay; live within your means; put by a nest egg for a rainy day; pay your bills on time; support the police.

1981

★

The National Health Service is safe with us … The principle that adequate healthcare should be provided for all regardless of ability to pay must be the function of any arrangements for financing the NHS. We stand by that.

Conservative Party Conference, October 1982

★

Some say I preach merely the homilies of housekeeping or the parables of the parlour. But I do not repent. Those parables would have saved many a financier from failure and many a country from crisis.

Lord Mayor's Banquet, 1982

★

The spirit has stirred and the nation has begun to assert itself. Things are not going to be the same again.

★

You can strike your way down, but you have to work your way up.

1983

★

Power is a trust and we must exercise it in that way.
9 June 1983

★

You can present people with ideas they may come to believe in, and as a result of them they will act, if they have the opportunities. Presenting people with opportunities is part of what politics is about.

★

If a political leader floats an idea five years ahead of its time he could kill that idea. But if it's two years ahead of its time it could work.

★

Young people ought not to be idle. It's very bad for them.
The Times, *1984*

★

I came to office with one deliberate intent – to change Britain from a dependent to a self reliant society, from a give it to me to a do it yourself nation, to a get up and go instead of a sit back and wait Britain.
The Times, *8 February 1984*

★

In the Conservative Party we have no truck with outmoded Marxist doctrine about class warfare. For us it is not who you are, who your family is or where you come

from that matters, but what you are and what you can do for your country that counts.
1984

★

Yes, unemployment breeds frustration, but it's an insult to the unemployed to suggest that a man who doesn't have a job is likely to break the law.
Conservative Party Conference, 11 October 1985

★

No one would remember the Good Samaritan if he'd only had good intentions. He had money as well.
1986

★

A responsible society is one in which people do not leave it to the person next door to do the job. It is one in which people help each other, where parents put their children first, friends look out for neighbours, families for their elderly members, that is the starting point for care and support – the unsung efforts of millions of individuals, the selfless work of thousands upon thousands of volunteers ... Caring isn't measured by what you say, it's expressed by what you do.
Conservative Women's Conference, 1986

★

Popular capitalism is on the march ... Of course, there will always be people who, in the name of morality, sneer at this and call it 'materialism'. But isn't it moral that people should want to improve the material standard of

living of their families, by their own effort? Isn't it moral
that families should work for the means to look after their
old folk? Isn't it moral that people should save, so as to be
responsible for themselves? ... And it is for government to
work with that grain in human nature to strengthen the
strand of responsibility and independence: it benefits the
family; it benefits the children; it is the essence of
freedom.
Scottish Conservative Party Conference, May 1987

★

It would be fatal for us to stand just where we are now.
What would be our slogan for the 1990s if we did that?
Would 'consolidate' be the word that we stitch on our
banners? Whose blood would run faster at the prospect of
five years of consolidation?
Speech to the Conservative Party Conference, 9 October 1987

★

Fear is not the basis for foreign policy.

★

Ours is a creed which travels and endures. Its truths are
written in the human heart. It is the faith which once
more has given life to Britain and offers hope to the world.
We pledge in this Party to uphold these principles of
freedom and to fight for them. We pledge it to our allies
overseas, and we pledge it to this country we are proud to
serve.
*The conclusion of Margaret Thatcher's final speech to a Conservative Party
Conference, 12 October 1990*

★

If you have a good Thatcher, you keep your home water
and wind-proof.
Interview with Barbara Walters, February 1991

★

Given time, it would have been seen as one of the most
far-reaching and beneficial reforms ever made in the
working of local government.
On the Community Charge (Poll Tax), 1993

Personality and Politics

You don't tell deliberate lies, but sometimes you have to
be evasive.
1976

★

I have changed everything.
1976

★

My great fear is that when the time comes, I might fail.
April 1977

★

I've got no hang-ups about my background, like you
intellectual commentators in the South East. When you're
actually doing things, you don't have time for hang-ups.
1977

★

There are a few times when I get home at night and everything has got on top of me when I shed a few tears, silently, alone.
1978

★

It is not the business of politicians to please everyone.
29 January 1978

★

The reason I am in politics is because I believe in certain things and try to put them into practice.

★

Being in power is like being a lady – if you have to tell people you are, you aren't.

★

We are not in politics to ignore people's worries, we are in politics to deal with them.

★

Many of our troubles are due to the fact that our people turn to politicians for everything.

★

If I lose, I will be out tomorrow.
Day before the 1979 election

★

Where there is discord may we bring harmony. Where there is error, may we bring truth. Where there is doubt, may we bring faith. Where there is despair, may we bring hope.
Quoting St Francis of Assisi on the steps of 10 Downing Street, May 1979

★

I hope the one quality I am not lacking is courage.
November 1979

★

I was on the Jimmy Young Show, he played an Andy Williams song for me and the song was 'The Other Side of Me'. Well there are two sides of me – the informal, friendly me and the iron touch, the Iron Lady.
Daily Mail, *May 1980*

★

I sort of regard myself as a very normal, ordinary person with all the right instinctive antennae.
Sunday Times, *3 August 1980*

★

I said at the start I shall get things right in the end, and I shall.
Daily Express, *August 1980*

★

To those waiting with bated breath for that favourite media catchphrase, the U Turn, I have only one thing to say. You turn if you want to. The Lady's not for turning.
Conservative Party Conference, 10 October 1980

★

Oh, those poor shopkeepers.
Visiting Toxteth after the 1981 riots

★

I do not believe that people who go on strike in this country have legitimate cause.
1982

★

'Oh, Lord, teach me to learn that occasionally I make mistakes.'
Quoting her favourite poem, BBC Radio, 1982

★

Victorian values were the values when our country became great.
1982

★

I was asked whether I was trying to restore Victorian values. I said straight out I was. And I am.
1983

★

I don't think I'm as good as you think.
1983

★

If you are going to work for politicians you should remember that they have very large fingers and very large toes and you can tread upon them remarkably easily. I, however, have stubs.

★

It's a result that will reverberate through our history. Its consequences will outlive most of us here tonight.
On the 1983 election result, 7 June 1983

★

It's got to be my ideas. Not every bit of draft is mine but I go through it all. First we do the ideas, they go away and draft, then that draft's usually torn up, then we do another one, and then I literally spend hours and hours going through that. We change it and change it, and some speeches we'd still be changing now, if we hadn't delivered them already.
On writing speeches, 9 June 1983

★

Cecil, these have been such happy hours. We have done such a lot for the country together and we will do much more.
To Cecil Parkinson following his resignation from the Government over the Sara Keays affair

★

If they do not wish to confer the honour, I am the last person who would wish to receive it.
On Oxford University's decision not to give her an honorary degree, 1985

★

I may not be Prime Minister at six o'clock.
To colleagues just before the no confidence debate over Westland, 26 January 1986

★

I know nothing about diplomacy, but I know I want certain things for Britain.
1986

★

There is just one thing I would like to make clear. The rose I am wearing is the rose of England.
A dig at Labour's red rose logo, Conservative Party Conference, 1986

★

I feel more genuine affection this time. I think I have become a bit of an institution and, you know, the sort of thing people expect to see around the place.
At the start of the General Election campaign, May 1987

★

I exercise my right as a free citizen to spend my own money in my own way, so that I can go on the day, the time, to the doctor I choose and get out fast.
On why she chooses to use private healthcare, causing a political storm during the General Election campaign, June 1987

★

Margaret Thatcher: If people just drool and drivel they care, then I turn round and say, right, I also look to see what you actually do.

David Dimbleby: Why do you use the words drool and drivel they care, is that what you think saying that you care about people's lives amounts to?
MT: No, I don't. I'm sorry I used those words.
Interview on the BBC 9 O'Clock News, 10 June 1987

★

We've got a big job to do in some of those inner cities, a really big job.
To Party workers at Conservative Central Office, 12 June 1987

★

Oh, I have lots of human weaknesses, who hasn't?
1987

★

We were told our campaign wasn't sufficiently slick. We regard that as a compliment.
1987

★

You cannot have my job and have had a vision, a dream, a will to turn Britain round, to live up to the best of herself, without being more than a chairman of a committee ... a Prime Minister has a task of leadership. If the trumpet gives an uncertain sound, who shall prepare himself to the battle? ... If one has a sense of purpose, they call that authoritarianism. It is totally false, but there you are ... Success is not an attractive thing to many people – they do not like it. And, of course, some of them are snobs. They can never forgive me for coming from a very ordinary background. It does not bother me at all. I cannot stand snobbery of any kind.
Interview with Brian Walden, Sunday Times, 8 May 1988

★

I'll stay until I'm tired of it. So long as Britain needs me, I shall never be tired of it.

★

Obviously one isn't indestructible – quite.
1988

★

I've seen and heard so many things on the BBC that infuriate me almost every day of the week – tendentious reporting, unfair comment, unbearable violence and vulgarity – that I hesitate to say yes when any part of the BBC asks me to do anything.
To George Urban, 29 June 1988

★

We have become a Grandmother.
To reporters outside 10 Downing Street, 1989

★

I am what I am.
29 November 1989

★

I don't expect gratitude. No politician should do that.
1990

★

Anything I want to keep quiet is normally in my handbag so it is not left lying around. Things do not leak from my handbag.
July 1990

★

One is an ordinary person, and don't you forget it!
To Eve Pollard, 1991

★

People who start things often don't see the end of them – take Moses and the Promised Land.
1992

★

I can be difficult and stubborn.
29 January 1994

Appearance and Lifestyle

You know how it is, if your hair looks awful, you feel awful.
Daily Mail, *July 1965*

★

I don't want to give my life over to politics. I don't think I'd have the ability and I'd never be given the chance.
On the possibility of becoming Prime Minister, Sunday Times, *March 1967*

★

Most of us have stopped using silver every day.
1970

★

I'm not hard, I'm frightfully soft, but I will not be hounded ... I can jolly well stick up for myself.
Daily Mail, *February 1972*

★

My hats seem to incense some people.
Daily Mail, *February 1972*

★

Do I look bedraggled, woebegone, in a state of shock? At some stage I shall have to go to Elizabeth Arden to have the ravages repaired, but do you see signs of shock in my face? It's easier for a woman than a man to give up power because you are not so lost. I can fill the time by spring-cleaning the house.
Daily Mail, *October 1974*

★

I'm a very good night worker.
1975

★

I married at 26. I knocked about a bit, as they say, and I was unhappy when my personal affairs did not go right. But I was never without hope for the future.

★

I am worried about my image. I'm going to change it ... I'm very aware that my image is important. I'm not at all pleased with the way I look on TV. I'm going to do something about it and the first thing is my hair. I'm going for the unkempt look.
Daily Mail, *May 1976*

★

I'm not as posh as I sound. I'm not grand at all.
Daily Mirror, *February 1977*

★

My greatest strength, I think, is that come what may I somehow cope.

★

I'm going to have furniture I like ... because I intend to be there a long time.
BBC Radio, *November 1977*

★

I do love an argument.
Daily Mail, *February 1980*

★

I couldn't live without work. That's what makes me so sympathetic to these people who are unemployed. I don't know how they live without working.
News of the World, *4 May 1980*

★

I sort of regard myself as very normal.

★

If you saw me at four o'clock in the morning with my make-up gone and running my hands through my hair you'd get a different picture.
August 1980

★

I haven't the figure for jeans.
1980

★

Failure? The possibilities don't exist.
On the Falklands War, 1982

★

Mr Parkinson, they tell me you have influence with the Prime Minister. She must take a proper holiday and if you will speak to her about it so will I!
Her Majesty the Queen to Cecil Parkinson, 1983

★

I'm sure I've made quite a number [of mistakes]. I don't think I could just suddenly say what they are now.
BBC Radio 4, 30 March 1983

★

Look at a day when you are supremely satisfied at the end. It's not a day when you lounge around doing nothing; it's when you've had everything to do and you've done it.

★

Of course it's the same old story. Truth usually is the same old story.

★

I am extraordinarily patient – provided that I get my own way in the end.
1989

Battle of the Sexes

If you want anything said, ask a man. If you want anything done, ask a woman.
May 1964

★

No woman in my time will be Prime Minister or Foreign Secretary – not the top jobs. Anyway I wouldn't want to be Prime Minister. You have to give yourself one hundred per cent to the job.
1969

★

I usually make up my mind about a man in ten seconds, and I very rarely change it.
1970

★

It will be years, and not in my time, before a woman will lead the Party or become Prime Minister.
1974

★

I owe nothing to women's lib.
Observer, *1 December 1974*

★

It may be the cock that crows, but it is the hen that lays the eggs.

★

I don't like strident women.

★

I like to be made a fuss of by a lot of chaps.
Daily Mirror, *February 1975*

★

I have a woman's ability to stick to a job and get on with it when everyone else walks off and leaves it.
16 February 1975

★

Part of me is a woman and part of me is a politician. The MPs voted for the whole of me.
February 1975

★

I cannot easily foresee the time when we have a woman Minister of Defence. But it would give me enormous joy to have the Navy singing There is Nothing Like a Dame.
April 1975

★

You cannot go so far up the ladder, and then not go to the limit, just because you are a woman.

★

One does wish that there were a few more women in Parliament. Then one could be less conspicuous oneself.

★

I don't notice that I'm a woman. I regard myself as the Prime Minister.
March 1980

★

Ronald Reagan: Margaret, he [Pierre Trudeau] had no business talking to you like that, he was way out of line.
Margaret Thatcher: Oh, women know when men are being childish.

★

The battle for women's rights has been largely won.
Conservative Party Conference 1982

★

One of the things being in politics has taught me is that men are not a reasoned or reasonable sex.

★

When a woman is strong she is strident. If a man is strong he is a good guy.
October 1990

★

Most women defend themselves – it is the female of the species – it is the tigress and lioness in you which tends to defend when attacked.

★

True gentlemen deal with others for what they are, not for who their fathers were.
BBC TV, 1993

★

In general, more nonsense was written about the so-called 'feminine factor' during my time in Office than just about anything else. I was always asked how it felt to be a woman Prime Minister. I would reply: 'I don't know, I've never experienced the alternative.'
Downing Street Years, 1993

★

My experience is that a number of the men I have dealt with in politics demonstrate precisely those characteristics which they attribute to women – vanity and an inability to make tough decisions. There are also certain types of men who simply cannot abide working for women ... Of course, in the eyes of the 'wet' Tory establishment I was not only a woman, but 'that' woman, someone not just of a different sex, but of a different class, a person with an alarming conviction that the values and virtues of middle England should be brought to bear on the problems which the establishment consensus had created. I offended on many counts.

Downing Street Years, *1993*

Denis and the Family

When Denis asked me to be his wife, I thought long and hard about it. I had so much set my heart on politics that I hadn't really figured marriage in my plans. I had pushed it to the back of my mind and assumed it would occur of its own accord at some time in the future. I know that Denis too, because his wartime marriage had ended in divorce, asked me to be his wife only after much reflection. But the more I considered it, the surer I was. There was only one possible answer.
Downing Street Years, *1993*

★

Denis's money got me on my way.
1983

★

She stood twice for Dartford and the second time she cried on my shoulder I married her.
Denis Thatcher

★

Denis has his own life and work and that's been very important to the both of us. He's not my second fiddle. He's first fiddle of his own orchestra. In fact he's his own conductor.
Daily Express, *20 February 1986*

★

I can trust my husband not to fall asleep on a public platform and he usually claps in the right places.

★

Several things, she's got a good pair of legs.
Denis Thatcher, in answer to a question on what attracted him to her

★

Tory Party worker: Mr Thatcher, I understand you have a drink problem.
Denis Thatcher: Yes, madam, I have. There is never enough of it.

★

Tory Party worker: Mr Thatcher, how do you spend your time?
Denis Thatcher: Well, when I'm not completely pissed I like to play a lot of golf.

★

If we're not careful, we'll have a dead cow on our hands.
Denis Thatcher during the 1979 general election campaign, when his wife picked up a baby calf for a photo opportunity

★

The desire to win is born in most of us. The will to win is a matter of training. The manner of winning is a matter of honour.
Denis Thatcher, quoted in Downing Street Years, *1993*

★

The Falklands marked her soul and mine.
Denis Thatcher

★

Congratulations Sweetie Pie, you've won. It's just the rules.
A tearful Denis Thatcher after the first round of the 1990 leadership election

★

Denis Thatcher: [in tears] It's just the disloyalty of it all.
Carol Thatcher: Look Dad, what really matters now is Mum. It's going to be a hell of a shock and we have to support her. We have to do everything we can to make it easier.
Walking across Horseguards Parade, 22 November, 1990

★

After all she's done, I think this is an act of gutless treachery. As far as I'm concerned Tory is now a four-letter word.
Carol Thatcher to a journalist outside her home, 22 November 1990

★

Oh Mum, it's me. I think you're a heroine [bursts into tears]. I don't know how you made that speech. It's just so awful what they've done – your party are complete shits.
Carol Thatcher, speaking to her mother on the evening of 22 November 1990

★

For forty years I have been married to one of the greatest women the world has ever produced. All I could produce – small as it may be – was love and loyalty.

★

Carol Thatcher: Can you manage the supermarket shopping?
Margaret Thatcher: Good heavens, yes, dear, I've opened enough of them.
December 1990

★

Isn't my mother wonderful, doing this for me and my son?
Mark Thatcher on his father's baronetcy, Mail on Sunday, 20 January 1991

★

Mark has a hate-hate relationship with the press. He feels the press for years and years has given him a very hard time. Quite frankly he can't stand them and he finds it hard to disguise it. Mark has the full confidence of his mother. She really trusts him. When you've been through what she went through, when a number of people whom you thought you could trust, proved not quite so trustworthy, then to have somebody in whom you have total trust, is vitally important, and I think Mark has filled a very important role for her.

Cecil Parkinson, World in Action, *11 November 1991*

★

It's time to pay up for Mumsy.

Mark Thatcher, raising money from businessmen to set up the Thatcher Foundation, 1991

★

Duchess of York: Oh Denis, I do get an awful press, don't I?
Denis Thatcher: Yes, Ma'am. Has it occurred to you to keep your mouth shut?

★

Being the only girl in the world who can say that her mother was Britain's first woman Prime Minister is honour enough for me.

Carol Thatcher, 13 June 1992

★

I now have to spell Thatcher when I make table reservations at restaurants – but I can cope with that.

Carol Thatcher, Independent, *28 December 1993*

★

The idea that I run around peddling Kalashnikovs or second hand MiG jets is ridiculous. I haven't even sold a penknife.

Mark Thatcher

★

You cannot think of Margaret without Denis. There comes a time when every Prime Minister needs someone to give him or her the unvarnished truth, and, in Denis, Margaret had just that.

John Major, October 1995

Fighting Socialism

I sometimes think the Labour Party is like a pub where the mild is running out. If someone does not do something soon, all that is left will be bitter and all that is bitter will be left.

1975

★

In a Socialist society, parents should be seen and not heard.

Conservative Party Conference, 10 October 1975

★

My job is to stop Britain going red.

The Times, *March 1977*

★

What would they [our ancestors] think of Labour Britain today? A country in which people ask: 'Why work if you can get by without?'; Why do a good job when you will probably make out just as well if you do a bad one?'; 'Why bother to get extra qualifications when differentials and earnings so often depend on political muscle, not personal merit?'

Conservative Party Conference, 13 October 1978

★

And what a prize we have to fight for: no less than the chance to banish from our land the dark, divisive clouds of Marxist Socialism.

Scottish Conservative Party Conference, May 1983

★

Socialism and Britain go ill together. It is not the British character.

Director *magazine, September 1983*

★

In the Falklands we had to fight the enemy without. Here the enemy is within and it is much more difficult to fight, but just as dangerous to liberty.

Speech to the 1922 Committee, referring to the miners, July 1984

★

What we've got is an attempt to substitute the rule of the mob, for the rule of the law. It must not succeed.

On the miners' strike, 1984

★

Scabs? They are lions!
On working miners, Conservative Party Conference, 13 October 1984

★

We were told you'll never stand a major industrial strike, let alone a coal strike. But we did just that. And we won.
Conservative Party Conference, 1985

★

We must take with us into the 1990s the lessons of the decade we are leaving behind. And the overwhelming lesson is that Socialism has failed.
January 1990

★

Beneath its contrived self-confidence lies a growing certainty that the world and history has passed it by and that if Britain rejects it as I believe it will, Socialism must return forever to its proper place – the reading room of the British Library where Karl Marx found it – Section: history of ideas. Subsection: nineteenth century. Status: archaic.
Conservative Party Conference, October 1990

Iron Lady

Every Conservative desires peace. The threat to peace comes from Communism which has powerful forces ready to attack anywhere. Communism waits for weakness, it leaves strength alone. Britain must therefore be strong, strong in her arms, strong in her faith, strong in her own way of life.

Margaret Roberts' election leaflet, 1950

★

Ladies and Gentlemen, I stand before you tonight in my green chiffon evening gown, my face softly made up, my hair softly waved ... The Iron Lady of the western world? Me? A cold warrior? Well, yes – if that is how they wish to interpret my defence of the values and freedom fundamental to our way of life.

Referring to the Soviet magazine Red Star *which was the first to call her the Iron Lady, 1976*

★

Perhaps this country needs an Iron Lady.
1977

★

Marxists get up early to further their cause. We must get up even earlier to defend our freedom.
Daily Mail, *May 1978*

★

Communism never sleeps, never changes its objectives. Nor must we.
Financial Times, *May 1979*

★

There are forces more powerful and pervasive than the apparatus of war. You may chain a man, but you cannot chain his mind. You may enslave him, but you will not conquer his spirit. In every decade since the war Soviet leaders have been reminded that their pitiless ideology only survives because it is maintained by force. But the day will come when the anger and frustration of the people is so great that force cannot contain it. Then the edifice cracks; the mortar crumbles ... one day, liberty will dawn on the other side of the wall.
In Berlin, 29 October 1982

★

We are prepared to fight for peace.
1983

★

We are the true peace movement.
1983

★

If you are pronouncing a new law that wherever Communism reigns against the will of the people, even though it's happened internally, there the United States shall enter, then we are going to have really terrible wars in the world.
Condemning the US invasion of Grenada, 1983

★

If in the 1930s nuclear weapons had been invented and the Allies had been faced by Nazi SS20s and Backfire bombers, would it then have been morally right to have handed Hitler control of one of the most terrible weapons man has ever made? Would not that have been the one way to ensure that the thousand year Reich became exactly that? Would not unilateralism have given to Hitler the world domination he sought?
1983

★

I first became interested in Communism from reading about it when I was 16 or 17. The thing which struck me very vividly was the total extinction of all personal liberty.

I saw then that they had a world objective – to dominate the world – which they pursued by one means or another. And this obviously never left me. It's not in the background of my mind, but in my bloodstream.

Daily Telegraph, *December 1983*

★

I am an ally of the United States. We believe the same things, we believe passionately in the same battle of ideas, we will defend them to the hilt. Never try to separate me from them.

To Mikhail Gorbachev at their first meeting in 1984.

★

The messages on our banners in 1979 – freedom, opportunity, family, enterprise, ownership – are now inscribed on the banners in Leipzig, Warsaw, Budapest and even Moscow.

O*ctober 1989*

★

What happened in Russia in 1917 wasn't a revolution – it was a coup d'etat.

Conservative Party Conference, 13 October 1989

★

I am in step with the people of South Africa.

October 1989

★

If we let Iraq succeed, no small country can ever feel safe again. The law of the jungle takes over.

August 1990

★

Human beings have their own rights as human beings and I will not sink to the level of using them as bargaining counters.
Responding to Saddam Hussein's imprisonment of western hostages, August 1990

★

In my view dictators do not surrender. They have to be well and truly defeated.
Independent on Sunday, *20 January 1991*

Falklands

Our judgement is that the presence of the Royal Marines garrison ... is sufficient deterrent against any possible aggression.
February 1982

★

If they are invaded, we have got to get them back.
To John Nott, 2 April 1982

★

The people of the Falkland Islands, like the people of the United Kingdom, are an island race. They are few in number but they have the right to live in peace, to choose their own way of life and to determine their own allegiance. Their way of life is British; their allegiance is to the Crown. It is the wish of the British people and the duty of Her Majesty's Government to do everything that we can to uphold that right. That will be our hope and our endeavour, and, I believe, the resolve of every Member of this House.

In the House of Commons, 3 April 1982

★

The Prime Minister, shortly after she came into office, received a sobriquet as the 'Iron Lady'. It arose in the context of remarks which she made about defence against the Soviet Union and its allies; but there was no reason to suppose that the Right Honourable Lady did not welcome and, indeed, take pride in that description. In the next week or two this House, the nation and the Right Honourable Lady herself, will learn of what metal she is made.

Enoch Powell, House of Commons, 3 April 1982

★

I don't want to fight any wars; if you can get them off before we get there, you do it, but off they go.

To General Alexander Haig, 8 April 1982

★

The British won't fight.

General Galtieri to Alexander Haig, 10 April 1982

★

Ah, François, it's you. You are with me.

To French President François Mitterrand, who had pledged his support in the Falklands conflict, April 1982

*

When you stop a dictator there are always risks, but there are great risks in not stopping a dictator. My generation learned that long ago.
1982

*

I'm standing up for the right of self-determination. I'm standing up for our territory. I'm standing up for our people. I'm standing up for international law. I'm standing up for all those territories – those small territories and peoples the world over – who, if someone doesn't stand up and say to an invader 'enough, stop' ... would be at risk.
Panorama, *BBC TV, 26 April 1982*

*

It is exciting to have a real crisis on your hands, when you have spent half your political life dealing with humdrum issues like the environment.
Scottish Conservative Party Conference, 14 May 1982

*

Gentlemen, I have spent the night thinking about this Peruvian [peace] initiative and I have to tell you that if is your decision to accept then you will have to find another Prime Minister.
To the War Cabinet, May 1982

*

The Government wants a peaceful settlement. But we totally reject a peaceful sell-out.
Scottish Conservative Party Conference, 14 May 1982

★

Just rejoice at the news and congratulate our armed forces and the Marines. Rejoice!
To journalists, following the retaking of South Georgia, May 1982

★

Ron, I'm not handing over ... I'm not handing over the islands now. I didn't lose some of my best ships and some of my finest lives to leave quietly under a ceasefire without the Argentines withdrawing.
To Ronald Reagan, 31 May 1982

★

[Admiral] Lewin would come in and give the bad news straight away. He said he was sorry but the *Sheffield* had been sunk. That was one of the occasions when she would put her head down and stare at the table and I felt had really withdrawn herself from the War Cabinet, for about a minute. Then she'd shake herself and come back in again, tears running down her face.
Sir Michael Havers, The Thatcher Factor, *Channel Four, 1990*

★

It shows that the substance under test consists of ferrous metal of the highest quality. It is of exceptional tensile strength, resistant to wear and tear, and may be used with advantage for all national purposes.
Enoch Powell explaining how the Iron Lady had stood up to the tests of the Falklands crisis

★

We have ceased to be a nation in retreat. We have instead a newfound confidence – born in the economic battles at home and tested and found true 8,000 miles away ... And so today, we can rejoice at our success in the Falklands and take pride in the achievement of the men and women of our task force. But we do so, not as some flickering of a flame which must soon be dead. No, we rejoice that Britain has rekindled that spirit which has fired her for generations past and which today has begun to burn as brightly as before. Britain found herself again in the South Atlantic and will not look back from the victory she has won.

3 July 1982

★

You were thinking every moment of the day about it, it was at the back of your mind no matter what else you were doing. You were thinking of what was happening down there and the decisions that had to be taken. When the telephone went or one of the duty clerks came up with a piece of paper in his hand, you always braced yourself as the thought raced through your mind, 'is this bad news?' I never had any doubt about the rightness of the decision. Even though we got the Task Forces there, there were voices saying, 'No, don't go and land, just negotiate'. I didn't go down there to negotiate. I went down there to get the Argentinians off and if they left then we didn't need to go into battle.

★

The spirit of the South Atlantic was the spirit of Britain at her best. It has been said that we surprised the world, that British patriotism was rediscovered in those spring days. It was never really lost. But it would be no bad thing if the feeling that swept the country then were to continue to inspire us. For if there was any doubt about the determination of the British people it was removed by the

men and women who, a few months ago, brought a renewed sense of pride and self-respect to our country.
Conservative Party Conference, 8 October 1982

★

She was a decisive leader, which of course is what the military want. We don't want somebody who vacillates, we want to be able to put the case to her, the requirements to her, and say this is how it is, this is the decision we want, we want it now and we want it quickly and we don't want a wishy-washy decision, we want a clear-cut decision. She was magnificent in her support of the military.
Admiral Terry Lewin, Chief of the Defence Staff during the Falklands crisis

★

Margaret Thatcher: Oh, arms to Argentina, you won't will you?
Ronald Reagan: No, we won't.
1987

Freedom

The legal system we have and the rule of law are far more responsible for our traditional liberties than any system of one man one vote. Any country or government which wants to proceed towards tyranny starts to undermine legal rights and undermine the law.

Conservative Party Conference, October 1966

★

Freedom under the law must never be taken for granted.

1975

★

I hope to be Prime Minister one day and I do not want there to be one street in Britain I cannot go down.

1 May 1977

★

Choice is the essence of ethics. If there were no choice there would be no ethics, no good, no evil. Good and evil only have meaning in so far as man is free to choose.
1977

★

If someone is confronting our essential liberties, if someone is inflicting injuries and harm, by God I'll confront them!
1979

★

We intend freedom and justice to conquer. Yes, we do have a creed and we wish others to share it. But it is not part of our policy to impose our beliefs by force or threat of force.
September 1983

★

We must try to find ways to starve the terrorist or the hijacker of the oxygen of publicity on which they depend.
Speech to the American Bar Association, 15 July 1985

★

Of course you have a duty to show the disfigurations of society as well as its more agreeable aspects. But if TV in the western world uses its freedom continually to show all that is worst in our society, while the centrally controlled television of the Communist world and the dictatorships show only what is judged advantageous to them and suppress everything else, how are the uncommitted to judge between us? How can they fail to misjudge if they view matters only through a distorted mirror?

To an audience of television producers

★

I am not one who, to quote an American author, believes that democracy and enterprise have finally won the battle of ideas – that we have therefore arrived at the end of history, and there is nothing left to fight for. That would be unutterably complacent, indeed foolish. There will always be threats to freedom, not only from frontal assaults, but more insidiously by erosion from within.

Independent, *14 November 1989*

★

I am an undiluted admirer of American values and the American dream and I believe they will continue to inspire not just the people of the United States but millions across the face of the globe.

Speech to the Aspen Institute, Colorado, 5 August 1990

Ireland

Northern Ireland is as British as Finchley.

★

If you wash your hands of Northern Ireland you wash them in blood.

Conservative Party Conference, 13 October 1978

★

Go back and tell everyone in the United States that this is what happens to the money they give to NORAID. Tell them not to send any more.

To two American tourists following the IRA bombing of the Chelsea Barracks, November 1979

★

I think that was an assassination attempt, don't you?

To speechwriter Ronnie Millar a few minutes after the IRA bomb went off in Brighton, October 1984

★

The bomb attack on the Grand Hotel early this morning was first and foremost an inhuman, undiscriminating attempt to massacre innocent, unsuspecting men and women staying in Brighton for our Conservative Conference. Our first thoughts must at once be for those who died and for those who are now in hospital recovering from their injuries. But the bomb attack clearly signified more than this. It was an attempt not only to disrupt and terminate our conference; it was an attempt to cripple Her Majesty's democratically elected Government. That is the scale of the outrage we have all shared, and the fact that we are gathered here now, shocked but composed and determined, is a sign not only that this attack has failed but that all attempts to destroy democracy by terrorism will fail.

Conservative Party Conference, 12 October 1984

★

In church on Sunday morning – it was lovely and we haven't had many lovely days – the sun was coming through the stained glass window and falling on some flowers. It just occurred to me that this was the day I was not meant to see. Then all of a sudden I thought 'there are some of my dearest friends who are not seeing this day'.

Following the IRA bomb attack on the Cabinet in Brighton, October 1984

★

Now it must be business as usual.

Outside Brighton police station following the IRA bombing of the Grand Hotel, 1984

★

I don't believe that the Prime Minister, when she said in 1979 'I'm a rock hard Unionist', was telling an untruth, I think she was correctly describing herself. She hated doing it. You only had to watch the Prime Minister in November 1985. She was a picture of misery. She just hated it. I suppose it is to her credit that having been convinced at that time that an overriding national interest was involved, she overrode her opinions, her wishes and her instincts.

Enoch Powell on the signing of the Anglo-Irish Agreement, The Thatcher Factor, *Channel 4, 1990*

★

All of a sudden, the world is broken.

Following the IRA assassination of Ian Gow, August 1990

★

It would be the equivalent of having the Prime Minister of England invite the Oklahoma City bombers to 10 Downing Street, to congratulate them on a job well done.

On President Clinton's welcome of Gerry Adams

My Style of
Government

We have made too much of one or two people, and we think that they can win or lose elections for us. Don't be depressed if one particular person transgresses. It doesn't lose an election unless the Party loses faith in itself.
July 1963

★

Power as a Minister doesn't give you power over the people. In the end, it's the people who have power over you.
Liverpool Daily Post, *February 1972*

★

I don't want a Cabinet of yes men or yes women. It's not healthy. I can't stand sycophants.
1977

★

I don't want a Cabinet of yes-men. They are no good to a Prime Minister.

★

There are two ways of making a Cabinet. One way is to have in it people representing the different points of view within the party, within the broad philosophy. The other way is to have in it only the people who want to go in the direction which every instinct tells me we have to go: clearly, steadily, firmly, with resolution. As Prime Minister, I could not waste my time having internal arguments.
1979

★

I am not a consensus politician – I'm a conviction politician.
1979

★

John Hoskyns [Head of Number Ten Policy Unit]: If there is ever to be any sort of U-turn on policy you absolutely must think about it now.
Margaret Thatcher: You know, I would rather go down than do that, so forget it.
1980

★

I don't mind how much my Ministers talk, as long as they do what I say.
1980

★

I love argument, I love debate. I don't expect anyone just to sit there and agree with me, that's not their job.
The Times, *1980*

★

The adrenalin flows when they really come out fighting at me, and I fight back and I stand there, and I know. Now come on Maggie, you are wholly on your own. No one can help you. And I love it!
1980

★

If you have conviction people are much more likely to come out and support you. Most of the great faiths upon which our own moral values are founded would never have got started if their prophets had gone out to the people and said: 'Brothers, I believe in consensus.
News of the World, *September 1981*

★

I will not change just to court popularity. Indeed, if ever a Conservative government start to do what they know to be wrong because they are afraid to do what they are sure is right, then is the time for Tories to cry 'Stop!' But you will never need to do that while I am Prime Minister.
Speech to the Conservative Party Conference, 16 October 1981

★

I am painted as the greatest little dictator, which is ridiculous – you always take some consultations.
The Times, *1983*

★

We want as many Conservatives as we can possibly get. I think I could handle a landslide all right.
In response to Francis Pym's assertion that large majorities can be dangerous,
June 1983

★

I'm a tough boss, yes I drive people, but it's my job to do that. But it's utterly ridiculous to call me a dictator.
1984

★

We got a really good consensus during the last election. Consensus behind my convictions.
1984

★

What is this thing called consensus? Consensus is something you reach when you cannot agree.

★

I go for agreement – agreement for the things I want to do.
The Times, *10 April 1984*

★

I don't spend a lifetime watching which way the cat jumps. I know really which way I want the cats to go.
1985

★

Obviously at sometime or other you have to hand over to someone new, fresh, young, dynamic. You do not want to cling on so they have to say: who is going to tell the old girl she had better go.
1985

★

I am the Cabinet rebel.

★

We believe a government's task is to give people the opportunity, not a handout.

★

Well I don't know why we are meeting. It is quite clear this matter must be settled and in fact I thought it was. So shall we just check some of the details?
As attributed to her by Kenneth Baker

★

I don't believe they [the voters] want a government to be so flexible it becomes invertebrate. You don't want a government full of flexi-toys.
1985

★

I sent them there to support me. They ought to know better.
On Conservative peers who voted against the Government

★

Margaret Thatcher: You will make no further statements or answer questions. This is the decision of the Cabinet and I must ask you to accept it.
Michael Heseltine: I cannot hesitate in supporting what I have said. There has been a breakdown of collective responsibility and I must therefore leave the Cabinet
9 January 1986

★

We have a style of great discussion and great debate. That has always been characteristic of my handling of government.
To American journalists, 18 January 1986

★

This is only the third time of asking. I hope to go on and on and on.
During the general election campaign, May 1987

★

I am staying my own sweet, reasonable self.
Following the resignation of Nigel Lawson, October 1989

★

You get a long way by nagging – nobody argued with me.
After the Dublin EC summit, March 1990

★

I think sometimes the Prime Minister should be intimidating. There's not much point being a weak, floppy thing in the chair, is there?
1993

★

I do not believe that collective responsibility is an interesting fiction, but a point of principle.
Downing Street Years, *1993*

★

I hated sacking Ministers and I could not prevent myself thinking what it meant to them and their families, suddenly losing salary, car and prestige.
Downing Street Years, *1993*

Sound Money

We should not underestimate the enormity of the task which lies ahead. But little can be achieved without sound money. It is the bedrock of sound government.
May 1979

★

Oh that Gilbert and Sullivan should be living in this hour. This [the Selective Employment Tax] is sheer cockeyed lunacy. The Chancellor needs a woman at the Treasury.
March 1966

★

It costs just as much to train a bad teacher as it does to train a good teacher.
1973

★

I do not believe it is in the character of the British people to begrudge the lion's share to those who have genuinely played the lion's part. They are ready to recognise that those who create the wealth – and I mean not only material but intellectual wealth – enrich the whole nation.
London Evening News, *September 1974*

★

Never in the history of human credit has so much been owed.
1975

★

Free enterprise has enabled the creative and the acquisitive urges of man to be given expression in a way which benefits all members of society. Let free enterprise fight back now, not for itself, but for all those who believe in freedom.
July 1975

★

There are too few rich and too few profits.
1975

★

When you take into public ownership a profitable industry the profits soon disappear. The goose that laid the golden eggs goes broody. State geese are not great layers.
1976

★

Our aim is to make tax collecting a declining industry.
Conservative Party Conference, 14 October 1977

★

Any woman who understands the problems of running a home will be near to understanding the problems of running a nation.
Observer, *8 May 1979*

★

We need to create a mood where it is everywhere thought morally right for as many people as possible to acquire capital.
July 1979

★

It is your tax which pays for public spending. The government have no money of their own. There is only taxpayers' money.
Conservative Party Conference, 12 October 1979

★

Pennies don't fall from heaven, they have to be earned on earth.
Sunday Telegraph, *November 1979*

★

We shall take whatever action is necessary to contain the growth of the money supply. The government, unlike so many of its predecessors, will face up to economic realities.
Speech to the Lord Mayor's Banquet, November 1979

★

We should not expect the State to appear in the guise of an extravagant good fairy at every christening, a loquacious companion at every stage of life's journey, the unknown mourner at every funeral.
March 1980

★

We have to get our production and our earnings in balance. There's no easy popularity in what we are proposing, but it is fundamentally sound. Yet I believe people accept there is no real alternative.
Conservative Women's Conference, 22 May 1980

★

What really gets me is this – it's very ironic that those who are most critical of extra tax are those who are most vociferous in demanding extra expenditure. What gets me even more is that having demanded that extra expenditure they are not prepared to face the consequences of their own action and stand by the necessity to get the tax to pay for it. I wish some of them had a bit more guts and courage than they have.
Referring to the Tory 'Wets', 1981

★

Economics are the method. The object is to change the heart and soul.
Sunday Times, *3 May 1981*

★

The secret of happiness is to live within your income and pay your bills on time.

★

A quick cure is a quack cure.
On unemployment, 27 May 1983

★

You can't buck the market.
On Chancellor Nigel Lawson's attempts to shadow the Deutsche Mark, 1989

★

I do wish I had brought my cheque book. I don't believe in credit cards.
At the Ideal Home Exhibition, March 1990

★

Everything a politician promises at election time has to be paid for either by higher taxation or by borrowing.
28 March 1992

Europe

Naturally, it is with some temerity that the pupil speaks before the master, because you know more about the Common Market than anybody.

To Edward Heath at a Keep Britain in Europe meeting, 1975. Mr Heath ignored her

★

I believe we should continue to have a partnership of national states each retaining the right to protect its vital interests, but developing more effectively than at present the habit of working together.

Conservative Party Campaign Guide, 1977

★

It has been suggested by some people in this country that I and my Government will be a 'soft touch' in the Community. In case such a rumour may have reached

your ears, Mr Chancellor ... it is only fair to advise you frankly to dismiss it, as my colleagues did long ago! I intend to be very discriminating in judging what are British interests and I shall be resolute in defending them.
Speech at a dinner in honour of German Chancellor, Helmut Schmidt, May 1979

★

We believe in a free Europe, not a standardized Europe. Diminish that variety within the member states, and you impoverish the whole Community. We insist that the institutions of the European Community are managed so that they increase the liberty of the individual throughout the continent. These institutions must not be permitted to dwindle into bureaucracy. Whenever they fail to enlarge freedom the institutions should be criticized and the balance restored.
July 1979

★

I have the money and they won't get their hands on it.
To Sir Nicholas Henderson, referring Britain's to EC budget contributions, 13 August 1979

★

They are all a rotten lot. Schmidt and the Americans and we are the only people who would do any standing up and fighting if necessary.
On fellow European leaders, 1979

★

I must be absolutely clear about this. Britain cannot accept the present situation on the budget. It is demonstrably unjust. It is politically indefensible. I cannot play Sister Bountiful to the Community while my own electorate are being asked to forgo improvements in the fields of health, education, welfare and the rest.

Winston Churchill Memorial Lecture, Luxemburg, 18 October 1980

★

I want my money back!

Dublin EC summit, November 1980

★

I can cope with nine of them, so they ought to be able to stand one of me. They could end the tiresomeness and stubbornness by giving me what I want.

The Times, *10 April 1984*

★

Mr Chairman, you have invited me to speak on the subject of Britain and Europe. Perhaps I should congratulate you on your courage. If you believe some of the things said and written about my views on Europe, it must seem rather like inviting Genghis Khan to speak on the virtues of peaceful co-existence.

Speech to the College of Europe, Bruges, 20 September 1988

★

My first guiding principle is this: willing and active co-operation between independent sovereign states ... Europe will be stronger precisely because it has France as France, Spain as Spain, Britain as Britain, each with its own customs, traditions and identity. It would be folly to try to fit them into some sort of identikit European personality.

Speech to the College of Europe, Bruges, 20 September 1988

★

We have not successfully rolled back the frontiers of the State in Britain, only to see them re-imposed at a European level, with a European Super-State exercising a new dominance from Brussels.
Speech to the College of Europe, Bruges, 20 September 1988

★

When the time is right.
The mantra for joining the European Exchange Rate Mechanism

★

Human rights did not begin with the French Revolution ... [they] really stem from a mixture of Judaism and Christianity ... [we English] had 1688, our quiet revolution, where Parliament exerted its will over the King ... it was not the sort of revolution that France's was ... 'Liberty, equality, fraternity' – they forgot obligations and duties I think. And then, of course the fraternity went missing for a long time.
Interview with Le Monde, *1989*

★

It took us a long time to get rid of the effects of the French Revolution 200 years ago. We don't want another one.
30 June 1989

★

To accuse Mrs Thatcher of wishing to torpedo Europe because she defends the interests of her country with great determination is to question her underlying

intentions in the same way that people used to question those of de Gaulle in regard to French interests.
Le Figaro, *November 1990*

★

It seems like cloud cuckoo land ... If anyone is suggesting that I would go to Parliament and suggest the abolition of the Pound Sterling – no! ... We have made it quite clear that we will not have a single currency imposed upon us.
October 1990

★

Yes, the Commission wants to increase its powers. Yes, it is a non-elected body and I do not want the Commission to increase its powers at the expense of the House, so of course we differ. The President of the Commission, Mr Delors, said at a press conference the other day that he wanted the European Parliament to be the democratic body of the Community. He wanted the Commission to be the Executive and he wanted the Council of Ministers to be the Senate. No! No! No!
Hansard, *30 October 1990*

★

All part of my vision of a wider Europe.
On the fall of the Berlin Wall, November 1990

★

A democratic Europe of nation states could be a force for liberty, enterprise and open trade. But, if creating a United States of Europe overrides these goals, the new Europe will be one of subsidy and protection.
Speech to the American Conservative Institutes, 8 March 1991

★

When will Labour learn that you cannot build Jerusalem in Brussels.
1992

★

If I were a German today, I would be proud, proud but also worried. I would be proud of the magnificent achievement of rebuilding my country, entrenching democracy and assuming the undoubtedly preponderant position in Europe. But a united Germany can't and won't subordinate its national interests in economic or in foreign policy to those of the Community indefinitely. Germany's new pre-eminence is a fact ... and its power is a problem – as much for Germans as for the rest of Europe.
15 May 1992

★

I pay tribute to John Major's achievement in persuading the other 11 Community heads of government that they could move ahead to the social chapter but not within the Treaty and without Britain's participation. It sets a vital precedent, for an enlarged Community can only function if we build in flexibility of that kind. John Major deserves high praise for ensuring at Maastricht that we would not have either a single currency or the absurd provisions of the social chapter forced upon us: our industry, workforce and national prosperity will benefit as a result.
15 May 1992

★

We weren't getting a fair deal on the budget and I wasn't going to have it. There's a great strand of equity and fairness in the British people – this is our characteristic.

There's not a strand of equity and fairness in Europe – they're out to get as much as they can. That's one of those enormous differences. So I tackled it on that basis.
BBC TV, 1993

★

If there is one instance in which a foreign policy I pursued met with unambiguous failure, it was my policy on German reunification.
Downing Street Years, 1993

★

It had the effect of cementing the Anglo-American alliance. What's the good of having bases if when you want to use them you're not allowed to by the home country. It made America realize that Britain was her real and true friend, when they were hard up against it and wanted something, and that no one else in Europe was. They're a weak lot, some of them in Europe you know. Weak. Feeble.
On the American air strike on Libya, BBC TV, 1993

★

We have been a little like an accomplice in a massacre. We cannot carry on like that.
On the West's role in Bosnia, 17 April 1993

★

The lesson of this century is that Europe will only be peaceful if the Americans are on this continent.
18 April 1993

★

In my day that would have required the occasional use of the handbag. Now it will be a cricket bat. But that's a good thing because it will be harder.
On John Major's negotiations on the Maastricht Treaty, 1993

★

I personally could never have signed this Treaty.
On the Maastricht Treaty, 12 June 1993

★

It is the people's turn to speak. It is their powers of which we are the custodians.
Calling for a referendum on the Maastricht Treaty, 17 July 1993

★

If Margaret Thatcher had been Prime Minister at the time, there would have been no Treaty of Maastricht.
Douglas Hurd, 6 November 1993

★

I was turned out because I said to Europe no, no, no. That no, no , no has now turned into yes, yes. Two yes's not three because he got the Social Chapter out and he's reserved his position on the single currency.
Interview with Sir David Frost, 1994

Wit, Wisdom and Regrets

Oh you are saucy!
To photographers, who had asked her to move closer to Canadian Prime Minister Pierre Trudeau

★

Ronald Millar: (giving her encouragement before her first speech to a Conservative Party Conference as Party leader) Piece of cake, Margaret.
Margaret Thatcher: Good heavens! Not now!
October 1975

★

Sydney Bidwell MP: Is the Right Honourable Lady aware that Mr Len Murray, the General Secretary of the TUC, insists that when he sees her, it is like having a dialogue with the deaf?

Margaret Thatcher: I had no idea that Mr Murray was deaf.

★

I confess that this is the biggest birthday party I have ever had. I just do not know whether my parents had in mind the timing of the party conference, but if that is what is meant by family planning I am all for it.

On her 53rd birthday at the Conservative Party Conference, 13 October 1978

★

James Callaghan: May I congratulate you on being the only man in your team.
Margaret Thatcher: That's one more than you've got in yours.

★

What do you think of those two then?
To male advisers, while holding up Page 3 of the Sun *in front of them*

★

Jim Prior: I read in my paper you had developed a sexy voice.
Margaret Thatcher: Jim, what makes you think I wasn't sexy before?

★

Here's the man who turned down a date with me.
To John Junor, after he had to turn down an invitation to Chequers

★

Don't worry dear, don't worry. It could happen to anyone.
To a Wren at Chequers who had just spilled gravy over Sir Geoffrey Howe

★

Michael Portillo: I have to be hard on you, Mrs Thatcher, because they will be. I have to be as tough as Fred Emery.
Margaret Thatcher: Oh, Michael, you're not like Fred Emery. He's not clever.
During the 1983 election campaign when the 25 year old Michael Portillo was a campaign aide

★

Will this thing jerk me off?
While firing a field gun during a visit to the Falkland Islands, January 1983

★

Ronald Reagan: Margaret, if one of your predecessors had been a little more clever ...
Margaret Thatcher: I know, I know, I would have been hosting this gathering.
At the 1983 Williamsburg Summit dinner

★

Denis Healey: You're going to cut and run.
Margaret Thatcher: The Right Honourable Gentleman is afraid of an election is he? He is frightened, frightened, frit!
1983

★

Senator Daniel P. Moynihan: Prime Minister, you have not disappointed us. You are the first person we have seen today who has offered us a real drink.
Margaret Thatcher: [Picking up a whisky] One can only take so much orange juice!
After Indira Gandhi's funeral, October 1984

★

I am always on the job.
Interview on Aspel and Co, LWT, 1984

★

Has he resigned or has he gone for a pee?
To Cabinet colleagues on Michael Heseltine's resignation, January 1986

★

I may be here, I may be twanging a harp.
Following a question from Sir Robin Day on whether she expected to still be Prime Minister in the year 2000, 12 June 1987

★

If it's one against forty-eight, I feel sorry for the forty-eight!
On the Commonwealth stance on South African sanctions

★

I am not quite certain what my Right Honourable Friend said, but we both hold precisely the same view.
In the House of Commons, January 1989

★

François Mitterrand: Shall we have a break now?
Margaret Thatcher: No, let's get on.
[The lights fuse and the room is plunged into darkness.]
Margaret Thatcher: Why can't we discuss the Social Chapter now?
At the EC Strasbourg summit, 1989

★

Kenneth Clarke: Isn't it terrible about losing to the Germans at our national sport, Prime Minister?
Margaret Thatcher: I shouldn't worry too much – we've beaten them twice this century at theirs.
Following England's loss to Germany in the 1990 World Cup soccer semi-final

★

Teacher to French primary school class: What is the name of the Queen of England?
Little girl: Elizabeth Thatcher?
Adapted from a letter to the Independent, *23 March 1990*

★

In the same period that the Americans have lived under one constitution our French friends notched up five. A *Punch* cartoon has a 19th century Englishman asking a librarian for a copy of the French constitution, only to be told: 'I am sorry sir, we do not stock periodicals'.
Speech to the American Conservative Institutes, 8 March 1991

★

Every Prime Minister needs a Willie.
On William Whitelaw, 1991

★

It was so hard on the daffodils
After a woman had hit her on the head with some daffodils, April 1992

★

I'm in a dreadful hurry this morning. I've really only got time to explode.
A rare example of self mockery to a group of her Ministers

★

Why don't you sit down? You look far too drunk to stand up!
To a Lords Whip

★

Margaret Thatcher: Did you ever practise at Chancery?
David Mellor: No.
MT: I thought so. Not clever enough.

★

Sir Robin Day: Can I get in this question please Prime Minister because ...
Margaret Thatcher: You asked me the most fundamental thing. I must beg of you.
RD: I know, but we're not having a party political broadcast, we're having an interview, which must depend on me asking some questions occasionally.
MT: Yes, indeed. You asked what I know you call the 'gut' question. Right, it's gone to the gut, it's gone to the jugular. Let me finish it.
Interview with Sir Robin Day, June 1987

★

TV interviewer: Do you ever say to Mr Kinnock: You did very well today, Neil?

Margaret Thatcher: No, I've never had occasion to say that.

★

Brian Walden: You come over as being someone who one of your backbenchers said is slightly off her trolley, authoritarian, domineering, refusing to listen to anybody else – why? Why cannot you publicly project what you have just told me is your private character?
Margaret Thatcher: Brian, if anyone's coming over as domineering in this interview, it's you. It's you.

★

Margaret Thatcher: Are you telling me that the Royal Navy ships out there will be under the command, of did you say a Belgian or a Dutchman?
Admiral Fieldhouse: Well, yes Prime Minister, they're our NATO allies.
Margaret Thatcher: A foreigner? The Royal Navy under the command of a foreigner?
Admiral Fieldhouse: NATO allies, Prime Minister. We operate together all the time.
Margaret Thatcher: A foreigner? The Royal Navy? Quite impossible!
Preparing for the Gulf War, September 1990

★

They [federalist European politicians] divide their time between court room, prison and debating chamber – giving a whole new meaning to the term conviction politician'.
Nicholas Ridley Memorial Lecture, 22 November 1996

★

We introduced the Community Charge. I still call it that. I like the Poles – I never had any intention of taxing them.
On the Poll Tax, Nicholas Ridley Memorial Lecture, 22 November 1996

Yes, Prime Minister

The following is the text of a *Yes, Prime Minister* sketch written and conceived by Margaret Thatcher's Press Secretary, Sir Bernard Ingham. The text was refined in consultation with the Prime Minister and her staff. It was performed by Margaret Thatcher, Paul Eddington (Jim Hacker) and Nigel Hawthorne (Sir Humphrey Appleby) in January 1984.

Margaret Thatcher: Good morning Jim, Sir Humphrey. Do come in and sit down. How's your wife? Is she well?

Jim Hacker: [*puzzled*] Oh yes, fine Prime Minister, fine thank you. Yes, fine.

MT: Good. So pleased. I've been meaning to have a word with you for some time. I've got an idea.

JH: [*brightening visibly*] An idea, Prime Minister? Oh good!

Sir Humphrey: [*guardedly*] An idea, Prime Minister?

MT: Well, not really an idea. I've done quite a bit of

thinking, and I'm sure you, Jim are quite the man to carry it out. It's got to do with a kind of institution and you are responsible for institutions aren't you?

Sir H: [*cautiously*] Institutions, Prime Minister?

JH: [*decisively*] Oh yes, institutions fall to me. Most definitely. And you want me to set one up, I suppose.

MT: Set one up? Certainly not, I want you to get rid of one.

JH: [*astonished*] Get rid of one, Prime Minister?

MT: Yes, it's all very simple. I want you to abolish economists.

JH: [*mouth open*] Abolish economists, Prime Minister?

MT: Yes, abolish economists – quickly.

Sir H: [*silkily*] All of them, Prime Minister?

MT: Yes, all of them. They never agree on anything. They just fill the heads of politicians with all sorts of curious notions, like the more you spend, the richer you get.

JH: [*coming round to the idea*] I take your point, Prime Minister. Can't have the nation's time wasted on curious notions, can we? No.

Sir H: [*sternly*] Minister!

MT: Quite right Jim. Absolute waste of time. Simply got to go.

JH: [*uncertain*] Simply got to go.

MT: [*motherly*] Yes, Jim. Don't worry. If it all goes wrong I shall get the blame. But if it goes right – as it will – then you'll get the credit for redeploying a lot of misapplied resources. Probably get promotion too.

Sir H: [*indignantly*] Resources? Resources, Prime Minister? Surely we're talking about economists.

MT: Were, Sir Humphrey. Were.

JH: [*decisively*] Yes, Humphrey, were. We're going to get rid of them.

MT: Well, it's all settled then. I'll look forward to receiving your plan for abolition soon. Tomorrow, shall we say? I'd like you to announce it before it all leaks.

JH: [*brightly*] Tomorrow then Prime Minister?

MT: Yes, well sort it out. Now, Sir Humphrey – what did you say your degree was?

Sir H: [*innocently*] Degree, Prime Minister?

MT: [*firmly*] Yes, Sir Humphrey, degree. Your degree. You have one, I take it – most permanent secretaries do – or perhaps two.

Sir H: [*modestly*] Er. Well actually, Prime Minister, a double first.

MT: Congratulations, Sir Humphrey, but what's it in?

Sir H: [*weakly*] Politics – er ... and, er ... economics.

MT: [*soothingly*] Capital, my dear Sir Humphrey. You'll know exactly where to start.

Sir H: [*bleakly*] Yes, Prime Minister

Sticks and Stones

During her political career, Margaret Thatcher was probably called more names and given more nicknames than any other living politician. What follows is but a small selection ...

Attila the Hen from Number Ten	Arthur Scargill
Bargain Basement Boadicea	Denis Healey
Baroness Belgrano	Edward Pearce
Boss	*Private Eye*
Catherine the Great of Finchley	Denis Healey
David Owen in drag	*Rhodesia Herald*
Egotistical Flea in a Fit	Neil Kinnock
Great She Elephant	Denis Healey
Grocer's Daughter	Valery Giscard D'Estaing
Heather	*Private Eye*
High Taxer Thatcher	Neil Kinnock
Iron Lady	*Red Star* newspaper (Moscow)
Iron Maiden	Marjorie Proops
La Passionara of Privilege	Denis Healey

Lady Macbeth	Roy Hattersley
Maggots Scratcher	Steven Berkoff
Man with Tits	Maureen Colquhoun
Mother	Tory MPs
Nanny of the Nation	Germaine Greer
Old Iron Knickers	Ron Brown
Parrot on Ronald Reagan's Shoulder	Denis Healey
Pétain in Petticoats	Denis Healey
Plutonium Blonde	Arthur Scargill
President Reagan's Glove Puppet	Gerald Kaufman
Rambina	Chris Buckland
Ramobona	Denis Healey
Rhoda the Rhino	Denis Healey
Surrogate Man	Glenys Kinnock
That Bloody Woman	Dennis Canavan
Thatch	Ben Elton
Thatcher – Milk Snatcher	The *Sun*
Thatchertollah	Neil Kinnock
The Blessed Margaret	Norman St John Stevas
The Immaculate Misconception	Norman St John Stevas
Thieving Magpie	Gerald Kaufman
TINA (There Is No Alternative)	*Private Eye*
Westminster Ripper	Dennis Skinner
Wicked Witch of the West	Gerald Kaufman
Winston Churchill in Drag	Denis Healey

According to Conservatives

The only occasion on which I thought it necessary to seek to guide her in the House was when she had scored in quick succession off [David] Marquand and [Richard] Crossman, and was joyfully following this up. I then said, 'Margaret, I know you are enjoying yourself, but do remember that the object is to get the Bill through!'
John Boyd Carpenter, Margaret Thatcher's Secretary of State at the Ministry of Pensions and National Insurance, 1961–62

★

This one is different. Quite exceptionally able, a first class brain.
Iain Macleod

★

Mark my words, Margaret Thatcher will be the next Leader of the Party.
Lord Margadale in 1972. His son, Peter Morrison, later became her Parliamentary Private Secretary

★

I have kissed her often before [but not] on a pavement outside a hotel in Eastbourne.
William Whitelaw, after a kiss for the benefit of reporters during the Conservative Party leadership election campaign, February 1975

★

It wasn't an election. It was an assumption.
Norman St John Stevas on her election as leader of the Party, 1975

★

In excluding me from the Shadow Cabinet Margaret Thatcher has chosen what I believe to be the only wholly honest solution and one which I accept and welcome.
Edward Heath, February 1975

★

I wouldn't say she was open minded on the Middle East so much as empty headed. For instance, she probably thinks that Sinai is the plural of sinuses.
Jonathan Aitken

★

We must create the new history for tomorrow's traditions.
Norman Strauss to Margaret Thatcher, 1977

★

I wouldn't treat my gamekeeper the way that woman treated me.
Christopher Soames following his sacking from the Cabinet, 1981

★

The trouble is, we've got a corporal at the top, not a cavalry officer.
Francis Pym

★

Prime Minister, you are talking too much.
A note from Lord Carrington to Margaret Thatcher during a meeting with the Chinese Prime Minister

★

She has provided the best leadership of any Prime Minister since Winston Churchill and she deserves the support of every patriotic citizen.
Reg Prentice, 1981

★

Margaret Thatcher and Ted Heath both have a great vision. The difference is that Margaret Thatcher has a vision that Britain will one day be great again, and Ted Heath has a vision that one day Ted Heath will be great again.
Robert Jones MP, 1981

★

She cannot see an institution without hitting it with her handbag.
Julian Critchley, 1982

★

I was struck by her incisiveness in everything she said and her grasp of her subject. She was never caught out, ever, by any question asked. So my recollection of her is quite clear. Curiously enough I came back one day and said to my wife, 'You know, she's got the brains of all of us put together, so we'd better look out'.
Lord Home on Mrs Thatcher in the Heath Government, 1985

★

Shut up, Prime Minister.
Nigel Lawson, after she continually interrupted Sir Keith Joseph at a Cabinet Meeting.

★

I think it was much more a peasants' uprising than a religious war. It was seen much more as the overthrow of the tyrant king rather than a great ideological shift.
Chris Patten on her election as leader of the Party, 1985

★

I tell you something she's not very good at; she's not very good at relaxing, taking time off. That's the nature of the creature. God Bless her, I think.
Sir Keith Joseph, 1985

★

I think Churchill would be appalled at the Thatcher Government.
Edward Heath

★

She's the only Party leader I can think of, certainly in the post-war period, who's been more radical in government than in opposition.
Chris Patten, 1985

★

Whatever the lady does is wrong. I do not know of a single right decision taken by her.
Edward Heath

★

To be loyal means 100 per cent acceptance of Government thinking: any dissent, or even admittance of doubt, is treachery and treason. After nine years as Party leader and five as Prime Minister, Margaret Thatcher still asks the question, 'Are you one of us?', by which she means, 'Are you completely free of any doubt as to the utter rightness of everything we are doing?' It will come as no surprise that I am not 'one of us'.
Francis Pym, 1986

★

Working with a team is not her strong point.
David Howell

★

She was like Boadicea, hammering away at those wicked people seeking to carry out policies alien to her trusted beliefs and nature.
James Prior

★

You've got to put her in the same category as Bloody Mary, Queen Elizabeth I, Queen Anne and Queen Victoria. However, she reminds me most of Queen Elizabeth I out of these four. Her handling of men is not dissimilar. I mean, if you had been a courtier of Queen Elizabeth I you would never have known quite whether you were going to get the treatment of an admired friend, or a poke in the eye with an umbrella.

Lord Hailsham

★

Although the advice that you get if you get to see Margaret is 'stand up for yourself, shout back, and argue the toss and then she will respect you', the trouble is that sort of advice to the English middle-class male of a certain age doesn't actually help us very much because we've always been brought up to believe that it's extremely rude to shout back at women.

Julian Critchley, 1985

★

Everyone likes to win arguments. She likes to win them more than most.

William Whitelaw, 1985

★

The truth of the matter is that in my experience she was almost always right and therefore there wasn't a great necessity for her to admit she was wrong.

Ian Gow

★

She is a very patient person. She can put up for a long time with being made to say what she doesn't believe.
Enoch Powell

★

I never thought of her as a woman.
John Biffen

★

She made up her mind really quite a long time ago that the country's future was damaged, really, by the trade unions, and she made up her mind to deal with that. And she made up her mind that inflation was the worst enemy of progress. And the two things, of course, were connected because trade union activities led to an increase in costs. And she did them both ... I think she felt her instincts were right and made up her mind to follow them, and in the course of that has done on the whole very well.
Lord Home, November 1988

★

History will surely recognize her achievements as Britain's first woman Prime Minister, a leader with the courage of her convictions, who assailed the conventional wisdom of her day, challenged and overthrew the existing order, changed the political map, and put her country on its feet again.
Sir Geoffrey Howe, May 1989

★

Tim Bell: It's up to you, you must tell her very firmly that she should stand down.
Gordon Reece: I can't. I love her.
Denis Thatcher: Steady on, she's my wife!
1989

★

She'll be Prime Minister until the middle of the next century.
Jeffrey Archer, 1989

★

Some people find it difficult to argue with a woman Prime Minister and shrivel up.
Douglas Hurd, BBC TV, 30 October 1989

★

I wish that old cow would resign.
Richard Needham, caught out on a mobile phone, 1990 – he later said sorry

★

May I say that my Right Honourable Friend the Prime Minister is looking jolly nice today?
Edwina Currie at Prime Minister's Questions just after announcing she thought the Prime Minister should retire, July 1990

★

She was at all times a politician and I was never entirely sure how much the saloon bar xenophobia of her later years represented her own uninhibited feelings and how far she saw it as a potential vote winner.
Nigel Lawson

★

On the issue of Europe Mrs Thatcher has very strong views and I understand those views. I do not share many of them.
Michael Heseltine, 17 November 1990

★

I am always there if she needs me and if I need her advice I would certainly approach her.
Gerald Bowden, Mrs Thatcher's local MP in Dulwich, December 1990

★

I was frequently embarrassed by the way Margaret conducted herself within the European Community. Her tactics were counter-productive and damaging to the UK's interests. On most issues her approach was foolish. Her style and tone of voice came to irk the others so much that they instinctively sank their differences and joined forces against her.
Nigel Lawson

★

She carried the cult of the individual much too far and has done us terrible damage in Europe with her fishwife yelling and screaming.
Nicholas Soames

★

Thatcherism is what you make of it. It was a knowledge that Butskellism did not work, but that one could not adopt market economics and patriotism without having a clear idea of what they entail. Thatcherism's mood was one of impatience with what was going on, the feeling that there were too many Old Etonians around. In the beginning was the mood, and the mood became Thatcher. It was essentially beliefs, not ideas.
Sir Alfred Sherman, April 1990

★

Not one of our economic achievements would have been possible without the courage and the leadership of the Prime Minister. And, if I may say so, they possibly derived some little benefit from the presence of a Chancellor who wasn't exactly a wet himself.
Sir Geoffrey Howe, Independent, *14 November 1990*

★

I am not running as Son of Margaret Thatcher. I have my own priorities and my own programmes.
John Major, The Times, *25 November 1990*

★

You don't have to leave Number Ten in tears.
Edward Heath, Independent on Sunday, *23 January 1990*

★

I've always had a great respect and been very candid with her, and I hope the reverse is the case.
Chris Patten, 1990

★

Margaret Thatcher drove us like there was no tomorrow. But I think there is a genuine feeling now that this macho, workaholic, earn lots of money way of life has run its course. There has been a shift in attitude. People are looking for a more balanced approach.

Edwina Currie on MPs' working hours, Independent on Sunday, *29 January 1991*

★

She is a formidable politician. She has always spoken her mind. She has a right to do it and she will continue to do so.

John Major, 29 June 1991

★

Anyone who supposed that when Margaret Thatcher left Number Ten she was going to take a Trappist vow did not know that formidable politician.

Chris Patten, December 1991

★

As Margaret Thatcher came up in the world, so the Conservative Party came down.

Julian Critchley, BBC TV, 1991

★

What has made her a Prime Minister whom so many of us admire is that she has a deep ideological sincerity. She believes. She is not there for herself at all. She is there because she believes we've got it all wrong in terms of ideology in this country. And she's right.

Lord Vinson

★

Mrs Thatcher was not lightly bullied.
Michael Heseltine, November 1991

★

Do you know what Margaret Thatcher did in her first budget? Introduced VAT on yachts! It somewhat ruined my retirement.
Edward Heath, 28 November 1992

★

Mrs Thatcher categorized her Ministers into those she could put down, those she could break down and those she could wear down.
Kenneth Baker, Independent, 11 September 1993

★

Was I ever one of us?
Kenneth Baker to Charles Powell, BBC TV, September 1993

★

She came to respect me, you know. She trusted me the longer I was there. I did some difficult things for her. I could deliver. I came to like her. I suppose I began to like her when she made me a Cabinet Minister. It was a very great honour.
Kenneth Baker, BBC TV, September 1993

*

We were all her creation.
Kenneth Baker, BBC TV, September 1993

*

It was like losing my mother. My mother is still alive but one day she won't be, and when that occurs it will, I suspect, be exactly like the day that Margaret Thatcher resigned.
Michael Brown, Daily Telegraph, *25 October 1993*

*

There were moments when Mrs Thatcher would privately rage so ferociously against something the Government had done that you almost forgot she was Prime Minister.
David Mellor, Independent, *4 March 1995*

*

I admired Margaret Thatcher hugely, but whenever you went near her, the stink of sycophancy was overwhelming. And she liked toffs, which I patently was not.
Steven Norris, 25 March 1995

*

She has the ability to see things from the grassroots level and know what is in people's minds.
Michael Portillo, 23 May 1995

*

The fact is that Margaret Thatcher was never really a Conservative.
Robert Rhodes James, 15 July 1995

According to Her
Opponents

The papers are full of Margaret Thatcher. She has lent herself with grace and charm to every piece of photographer's gimmickry, and don't we all when the prize is big enough? What interests me now is how blooming she looks. She has never been prettier. I am interested because I understand this phenomenon. She may have been up late on the Finance Bill Committee, she's beset by enemies but she sails through it looking her best. I understand why – she's in love – in love with power, success and herself.
Barbara Castle's diary, 5 February 1975

★

You know there are times, perhaps once every thirty years, when there is a sea-change in politics. It then does not matter what you say or what you do. There is a shift in

110

what the public wants and what it approves of. I suspect there is now such a sea-change and it is for Mrs Thatcher.
James Callaghan, just prior to Mrs Thatcher's election victory, May 1979

★

I can well understand the anxieties and pressures that must have been upon you during these weeks and I can understand that at this moment these pressures and these anxieties may be relieved, and I congratulate you.
Opposition leader Michael Foot following the retaking of the Falklands, June 1982

★

Although we were not displeased in the Labour lady members' room when Margaret Thatcher got the Opposition leadership, we knew that she was what the American feminists irreverently call 'a man with tits' and would do little or nothing either for women in the House [of Commons] or women outside it.
Maureen Colquhoun MP

★

To talk of Mrs Thatcher glorying in Falklands slaughter is to move the politics of the gutter to the politics of the abattoir.
David Owen, after Denis Healey had accused her of glorifying in slaughter, 2 June 1983

★

If Margaret Thatcher wins on Thursday, I warn you not to be ordinary, I warn you not to be young, I warn you not to fall ill, and I warn you not to grow old.
Neil Kinnock, 7 June 1983

*

She is the Castro of the western world – an embarrassment to all her friends. All she lacks is the beard.
Denis Healey

*

Some say Mrs Thatcher has a soft spot for the Nottinghamshire miners. But she is like one of those insects that consumes its mate after it has done the business.
Frank Dobson

*

Personally I think that she has the qualities of a very great politician. I believe she has tremendous conviction, she has drive, she has a commitment, she is totally genuine.
Michael Meacher, 1985

*

Mrs Thatcher has a great sense of propriety and she believes, as many women from her particular class believe, and certainly women with important positions believe, that it's part of their duty to be solicitous and kindly in an official way, and she is fastidious in following that through.
Neil Kinnock, 1985

*

She adds the diplomacy of Alf Garnett to the economics of Arthur Daley.
Denis Healey

★

She believes she can treat TV interviewers just like her Cabinet.
Donald Anderson

★

Ted Heath in drag.
Denis Healey

★

I'm entirely in favour of Mrs Thatcher's visit to the Falklands. I find a bit of hesitation though, about her coming back.
John Mortimer

★

She has fought resolutely for the class she represents and there are some lessons we might learn from that.
Tony Benn

★

That appalling woman.
Neil Kinnock

★

I cannot bring myself to vote for a woman who has been voice-trained to speak to me as though my dog has just died.
Keith Waterhouse

★

We are definitely in for the last few weeks of Thatcherism – the last few weeks of that job-destroying, oil-wasting, truth-twisting, service-smashing, nation-splitting bunch of twisters under a one person government.
Neil Kinnock, May 1987

★

She only went to Venice because somebody told her she could walk down the middle of the street.
Neil Kinnock on Mrs Thatcher's trip to the Venice economic summit during the General Election campaign, 9 June 1987

★

How do we know that next time, as always in the past, when President Reagan says jump, she will not reply 'How high?'
Denis Healey

★

I have never considered Margaret Thatcher to be a Tory. In some senses she is a populist, she's an instinctive politician, she's not afraid of change, she's not afraid to challenge vested interests and doesn't mind if they are Tory interests – this is where she has an appeal. You cannot deny her political acumen and skills.
David Owen, May 1988

★

When I hear the Prime Minister feeling sorry for the rest of the world, I understand why she has taken to calling herself 'we' – it's less lonely that way.
Neil Kinnock

★

Mrs Thatcher will go down in history as one of the great Prime Ministers of this country.
Paddy Ashdown, 1988

★

She is happier getting in and out of tanks than in and out of museums or theatre seats. She seems to derive more pleasure from admiring new missiles than great works of art. What else can we expect from an ex spam hoarder from Grantham, presiding over the social and economic decline of the country.
Tony Banks

★

The Prime Minister tells us that she has given the French President a piece of her mind – not a gift I would receive with alacrity.
Denis Healey

★

Trying to tell the Prime Minister anything is like making an important phone-call and getting an answering machine.
David Steel

★

She is about as environmentally friendly as the bubonic plague. I would be happy to see Margaret Thatcher stuffed, mounted, put in a glass case and left in a museum.
Tony Banks

★

She is a heady mix of whisky and perfume.
David Owen

★

Yesterday was hers, tomorrow is ours.
Neil Kinnock, on the tenth anniversary of her election, May 1989

★

I'd rather kiss Mrs Thatcher.
Brian Clough, denying he was retiring, 25 October 1989

★

It is now clear that the Prime Minister intends to become the Ceauşescu of the west and the main function of the Tory chairman at the next Party Conference will be to arrange 69 standing ovations for her.
Denis Healey, November 1989

★

I often compare the Prime Minister with Florence Nightingale. She stalks through the wards of our hospitals as a lady with a lamp – unfortunately it's a blowlamp.
Denis Healey

★

I think she may need to put up a tough appearance to compensate for the fact she is not a man.
Andrew Faulds MP

★

She believes in something. It is an old fashioned idea.
Tony Benn

★

The trouble is, she's like Maradona – always arguing with the referee.
David Owen, August 1990

★

Papua New Guinea is the only other country with a poll tax. The time has come for the Tory Party to conclude that Mrs Thatcher could serve Great Britain best as our ambassador there.
Robin Cook, March 1990

★

She is a half mad old bag lady. The Finchley whinger. She said the poll tax was the government's flagship. Like a captain she went down with her flagship. Unfortunately for the Conservative Party she keeps bobbing up again. Her head keeps appearing above the waves.
Tony Banks

★

Mrs Thatcher likes to portray herself as Mother Earth. To the poor children of this country she is Mother Hubbard and her cupboard is always bare.
Joan Lestor, October 1990

*

The problem for the Conservatives is that they were damned with Mrs Thatcher but are also damned without her.
Bryan Gould, 8 January 1991

*

A lot of what Mrs Thatcher did I only blame her in part for. I blame [the Cabinet] for letting her get away with it.
Neil Kinnock, 11 May 1991

*

You could fire a bazooka at her and inflict three large holes. Still she kept coming.
Roy Hattersley on her performance at Prime Minister's Question Time, October 1991

*

When you hear that Mrs Thatcher is going to become Countess of Finchley, that certainly adds impetus to abolishing the House of Lords.
Charles Kennedy, October 1991

*

I'm the sort of person Mrs Thatcher's parents warned her not to talk to as a little girl. I'm quite proud of that.
Ken Livingstone, 8 July 1995

According to Foreign Leaders

She is trying to wear the trousers of Winston Churchill.
Leonid Brezhnev, 1979

★

I couldn't be happier than I am over England's new Prime Minister ... I've been rooting for her to become Prime Minister since our first meeting. If anyone can remind England of the greatness it knew during those dangerous days of World War II when alone and unafraid her people fought the Battle of Britain it will be the Prime Minister the English press has already nicknamed 'Maggie'.
Ronald Reagan, June 1979

★

Somebody get me a stiff drink. That's a hell of a tough lady.
General Alexander Haig after a meeting with Mrs Thatcher during the Falklands crisis, April 1982

★

World affairs today demand the boldness and integrity of a Churchill. In his absence, I know he would want us to look to you as the legendary Britannia, a special lady, the greatest defender of the realm.
President Reagan, September 1983

★

The best man in Britain.
President Reagan, 1983

★

On more than one occasion I said to him, Mr President, if you do that, Margaret Thatcher is going to be on the phone in an instant. And he said: 'Oh I don't want that'.
Frank Carlucci on Ronald Reagan

★

If I were married to her, I'd be sure and have the dinner on the table when she got home.
George Schultz, US Secretary of State, 1982-89

★

She has the eyes of Caligula, but the mouth of Marilyn Monroe.
François Mitterrand, briefing his new Foreign Minister, Roland Dumas

★

As I prepare to depart this Office in January I take considerable satisfaction in knowing that Margaret Thatcher will still reside at Number Ten Downing Street and will be there to offer President Bush her friendship, cooperation and advice. She's a world leader in every meaning of the word.
President Reagan, December 1988

★

Mrs Thatcher, who can be so tough when she talks to her European partners, is like a little girl of eight years old when she talks to the President of the United States. You have to cock your ear to hear her, she's really so touching.
François Mitterand, 1989

★

We know that God has endowed her with that great quality of not fidgeting when it is necessary to come to grips with prickly nettles ... Mrs Thatcher epitomizes that something extra in womanhood. Mrs Thatcher enhances the meaning of womanhood.
Mangosuthu Buthelezi, October 1989

★

The courage to state her case and side with the majority of black South Africans against a hostile and uninformed international community is the kind of courage which history only produces on rare occasions.
Mangosuthu Buthelezi, March 1990

★

We don't all have the same warmongering ardour she is capable of at times.
Felipe Gonzalez, August 1990

★

Jesus, in Canada we erect a monument to a chap who loses three elections. In Britain you threaten to get rid of your Prime Minister when she wins three. What on earth is going on?
Brian Mulroney to Sir Bernard Ingham, 19 November 1990

★

I liked her immediately. She was warm, feminine, gracious and intelligent, and it was evident from our first words that we were soul mates when it came to reducing government and expanding economic freedom.
Ronald Reagan, 1990

★

For us she is not the Iron Lady. She is the kind, dear Mrs Thatcher.
Alexander Dubcek

★

She pulled her notes out of her famous handbag. These were the prepared subjects for our talk. I got my folder full of notes, then the conversation began. And you know I felt that she was dropping those damned prepared topics. She put her notes in her handbag and pushed it away, and we simply began to talk., to argue, to discuss. I felt the same thing that she felt, that there was no hindrance to being able calmly to consider the most difficult questions.

Mikhail Gorbachev on their first meeting in 1984, BBC TV, 1993

★

The difference between us is that I am living after Winston Churchill and she comes from the time before Winston Churchill.

Helmut Kohl, 16 October 1993

According to the Rest

A young woman of decided convictions.
Grantham Journal, *July 1945*

★

[Mrs Thatcher] sounds as though she is always wearing a hat.
1970

★

The most unpopular woman in Britain.
The Sun, *25 November 1971*

★

The Tories need more men like her.
Frank Johnson, Daily Telegraph, *November 1974*

★

Mrs Thatcher's Shadow Cabinet does credit to Mrs Thatcher herself. This Shadow Cabinet is not notably to the right of the previous one. Indeed, if anything, it gives stronger positions of influence to the conservatism of compassion.
The Times, *February 1975*

★

Margaret Thatcher's great strength seems to be the better people know her, the better they like her. But of course she has one great disadvantage. She is a daughter of the people and looks trim, as the daughters of the people desire to be.
Dame Rebecca West, Sunday Times, *25 July 1976*

★

I think that very few people on the *Sunday Times* were, by disposition or condition, pro her. We all thought she was a rather bossy, hand-baggy sort of lady. Already, that's the way we felt. But by the end of the lunch, she had argued so well, was so much in control of her facts, never lost her cool, and never let anybody get away with anything without pinning it down, and carried it off so well, that everyone around the table in their different ways was impressed.
Frank Giles, January 1990

★

If she has a fault, it is being too tender-hearted.
Paul Johnson, 1977

★

Perhaps I am a bit in love with Mrs Thatcher – platonically of course.
Woodrow Wyatt, 1977

★

There is no side about her. She does not put on airs or assert herself. She is not aggressive or cocky. Nor is she like Barbara Castle who always seems to be trying to mark her personality on the occasion.
Sir Nicholas Henderson, December 1977

★

Mrs Thatcher actually believes what she says and intends to act in a way consistent with her utterances if and when she becomes Prime Minister.
Ian Aitken, March 1978

★

Don't be afraid to give her your advice. And don't be afraid to interrupt her or you'll never give that advice.
Sir Jack Rampton to Sir Bernard Ingham, September 1979

★

She is the Enid Blyton of economics. Nothing must be allowed to spoil her simple plots.
Richard Holme, 10 September 1980

★

Margaret Thatcher is now awesome. No longer just a national figure. She's inexorably turning into a bronze monument of herself. She is living out a legend in the Falklands which will go down in history.
Jean Rook, Daily Express *columnist and First Lady of Fleet Street, 1983*

★

Hilda's Personal Photographer.
Slogan on T-shirts worn by photographers accompanying Mrs Thatcher on the final day of the 1983 election campaign

★

Thatcherism is not an ideology, but a political style: a trick of presenting reasonable, rather pedestrian ideas in a way that drives reasonable men into a frothing rage.
Andrew Brown, The Spectator, *1984*

★

She's the only person I know who I don't think I've heard say, 'I wonder whether'.
Sir William Pile, 1985

★

Thatcher had just become Prime Minister; there was talk whether it was an advance to have a woman Prime Minister if it was someone with policies like hers: she may be a woman but she isn't a sister. She may be a sister but she isn't a comrade.
Caryl Churchill, 1987

★

... it may well be that economic Thatcherism [stressing the importance of freedom and competition] would not be indefinitely acceptable to the British public unless there appeared to be a broader social dimension [stressing the importance of responsibility and morality] as well.
Geoffrey Smith, The Times, *1988*

★

A few years ago, in an after dinner speech, I cracked a little joke about going to Number 10 and beginning my interview thus: 'Prime Minister, what is your answer to my first question?'. Among those who laughed loudest were several members of Mrs Thatcher's Cabinet.
Sir Robin Day, 1989

★

Nobody could have fought through the spoken and unspoken prejudice of the Fifties, the giggles and sneers of the Sixties, and the concealed male resentment and subtle male condescension of the Seventies and Eighties, without bearing the scars ... An outsider to her Party cannot know what she has to put up with.
Matthew Parris, The Spectator, *15 April 1989*

★

She has a pretty face, hasn't she? I expect she's pretty tough. Her great virtue is saying that two and two makes four, which is unpopular nowadays as it always has been. I adore Mrs Thatcher. At last politics make sense to me, which it hasn't since Stafford Cripps.
Philip Larkin

★

One is, on the whole, glad that she is there, and we are here.
American columnist William Pfaff

★

If I request that someone pass me the mustard, I do not get it until I have been told how obnoxious the Thatcher woman is. Hatred of Mrs Thatcher seems to have become

obsessively implanted in the minds of the chattering classes and provides them with their principal source of conversation.
Brian Walden, 27 August 1989

★

Mrs Thatcher gained power at a time when it seemed that the collective was depriving the individual of responsibility for his own life. Even crime was no longer an individual act: it was a response to social conditions [a view which insulted all decent people living in the same conditions but abstaining from criminal activity]. She disagreed ... To dramatize this, she insisted 'society did not exist', though it was against an exaggerated view of society that she was reacting. Nothing she said would have been denied by Protestant churchmen before this century.
Allan Massie, Sunday Times, *1989.*

★

Very like interviewing a telephone answering machine. You pose a question, you get an answer, and then you start to make a response and you find it's just going on and on and on.
Peter Jay on interviewing Margaret Thatcher

★

The world shares our happiness – only Maggie continues to nag and scold.
Bild Zeitung *on German reunification, February 1990*

★

She's taken over from the Queen as someone who I dream about.
Kingsley Amis, Independent, *25 March 1990*

★

One of the best looking women I have ever met.
Kingsley Amis

★

There is no one who is ever going to convince me that this is not a woman who is caring and compassionate and fiercely loyal to her friends.
Sir John Junor, 1990

★

Came the 1960s and 1970s: corporatism, planning, protectionism and buttering up vested interest were tried by Conservative governments as well as Labour, and failed. One or two Tories – Enoch Powell, Keith Joseph – began to look again at the laissez-faire tradition, and so did Margaret Thatcher. Of course, she has never been a true Manchester liberal ... Her own politics are rather those of Lord Copper and the Daily Beast, 'self-sufficiency at home, self-assertion abroad', and this combination of *enrichez vous* and populist nationalism has made her in electoral terms the most successful party leader of the century.
Geoffrey Wheatcroft, Encounter, *1990.*

★

Like interviewing the Niagara Falls – magnificent, unstoppable.
Ann Leslie, Daily Mail

★

It is possible that she has accomplished what God sent her on Earth to do.
Mary Kenny, Independent on Sunday, *11 March 1990*

★

Both Margaret Thatcher and Keith Joseph had the courage of their convictions, but in a sense it was he who provided the convictions to match her courage.
Morrison Halcrow

★

She was nice and cuddly.
Paul Gascoigne, following a Downing Street reception for the 1990 World Cup squad

★

[She is] no puny leader, shaking a derisory fist as her enemies gather for the kill. Her self-image gives her a mighty stature, and she conveys this with every word of defiance she utters.
Hugo Young, Guardian, *22 November 1990*

★

A man can forgive a woman anything except having greater reserves of testosterone than he does.
Wesley Pruden, Washington Times, *20 November 1990*

★

She's too damn good for them.
Daily Mail *headline, 23 November 1990*

★

The oddity about the Thatcher years is that the liberal influence has waxed rather than wanted.
Lord Deedes, 21 September 1991

*

Mrs Thatcher is not uncaring or cruel, but she is naïve. She can't comprehend how absolutely useless, helpless and hopeless a good many people are, and is cursed with an incredible optimism and romanticism as to what the individual is capable of. If she kicks away the crutches, it's because she really does believe that everyone has the ability to walk without them.
Julie Burchill, 1992

*

A big cat detained briefly in a poodle parlour, sharpening her claws on the velvet.
Matthew Parris on Lady Thatcher in the House of Lords, Look Behind You!, *1993*

*

You can't keep a good diva down.
Nancy Banks-Smith

*

The Iron Lady wasn't perfect, critics of John Major are muttering, but at least she had lead in her pencil.
Rosalind Coward, Guardian, *6 October 1993*

*

It helps if Mrs Thatcher, as she proceeds with her unassailable argument, progresses physically further and further across the sofa until she is practically upon the interviewer.
Terry Coleman on interviewing Margaret Thatcher, Guardian, *6 November 1993*

★

Those of us who write about these things should admit that Margaret Thatcher's *Downing Street Years* was a far better book than we expected. It reads well and is often gripping. It is one-sided, self confident, insincere, single-minded, selective, deeply unfair and rather magnificent – like its author. The book's authenticity may be questioned but the unwitting picture of her will endure.

Stephen Spender, Sunday Telegraph, *12 December 1993*

★

You don't look too bad at all.

John Humphrys just before interviewing her, 11 July 1995

★

I was in love with her, yes, but I suppose in the best platonic manner, because, well, she was a marvellous girl. At that time, well, she still can – she looked rather beautiful. But her skin was glowing and she had very fine legs.

Woodrow Wyatt, Independent on Sunday, *November 1996*

★

We are true Thatcherites. She was the first Spice Girl, the pioneer of our ideology, girl power. What matters in life is the ability to rise and do anything ... I like the woman. Even if her policies were hard-headed, Socialism is bad.

Geri of the Spice Girls, Sun, *13 December 1996*

★

Mrs Thatcher used to be like one of the lions in Trafalgar Square. Malcolm Rifkind is like one of the pigeons.

Dr Alan Sked, leader of the UK Independence Party, 16 December 1996

On Conservatives

I'll always be fond of dear Ted, but there's no sympathy in politics.
On former Prime Minister Edward Heath, 1975

★

They broke Keith, but they won't break me.
On Sir Keith Joseph, January 1975

★

When I look at him [Edward Heath] and he looks at me, I don't feel that it is a man looking at a woman. More like a woman being looked at by another woman.
To Sir John Junor, 1979

★

We all make mistakes now and then. I think it was a mistake, and Jim Prior was very, very sorry indeed for it, and very apologetic. But you don't just sack a chap for one mistake.

On Jim Prior, following his criticism of the British Steel management, 21 January 1980

★

I got the distinct impression that he felt he was being dismissed by his housemaid.

On the dismissal of Christopher Soames from her Cabinet, 1981

★

The trouble with you is you talk too much. You remind me of Robert Carr.

On Kenneth Clarke [as reported by Kenneth Baker]

★

Keith and I have no toes.

On Sir Keith Joseph

★

He supported me steadfastly when I was right, and, more important, when I wasn't.

On William Whitelaw, Downing Street Years, *1993*

★

Others bring me problems, David brings me solutions.

On David [later Lord] Young, 1990

★

He thinks in paragraphs.
On Lord Cockfield

★

The trouble with Nigel is that he's a gambler.
On Nigel Lawson

★

He has given this country great service. He is the only one who really thinks the same way as I do.
On Cecil Parkinson, 9 April 1986

★

The thing about us Bernard is that neither of us are smooth people.
To Bernard Ingham

★

I was told that Bernard's politics had been Labour, not Conservative; but the first time we met I warmed to this tough, blunt, humorous Yorkshireman. Bernard's outstanding virtue was his total integrity. An honest man himself, he expected the same high standards from others. He never let me down.
Downing Street Years, *1993*

★

My Foreign Secretary said if I didn't commit myself to a date, he'd resign. Well I didn't commit myself, and he hasn't resigned. What sort of Foreign Secretary have I got?

On Sir Geoffrey Howe after the Madrid summit, referring to a commitment to join the Exchange Rate Mechanism, July 1989

★

He is another one of us.
On John Major, 1989

★

John Gummer just did not have the political clout or credibility to rally the troops. I had appointed him as a sort of nightwatchman, but he seemed to have to sleep on the job.
On John Gummer's period as Chairman of the Conservative Party, Downing Street Years, 1993

★

He was the extrovert's extrovert. He had prodigious energy; he was and remains the most popular speaker the Party has ever had ... Unfortunately, as it turned out, Jeffrey's political judgement did not always match his enormous energy and fund-raising ability: ill-considered remarks got him and the Party into somewhat awkward scrapes, but he always got himself out of them.
On Jeffrey Archer, Downing Street Years, 1993

★

Geoffrey was regularly bullied in debate by Denis Healey. But by thorough mastery of his brief and an ability to marshal arguments and advice from different sources, he had shown that beneath a deceptively mild exterior he had the makings of the fine Chancellor he was to become. Some of the toughest decisions were to fall to him. He never flinched. In my view, these were his best political years.

On Sir Geoffrey Howe, Downing Street Years, 1993

★

Nigel was secretive. I think he was a man of many complexes, he was also a man of many, many talents, sometimes a very creative person will also have great drawbacks. He did some very imaginative Budgets in income tax. He wrote the best Budgets as far as style is concerned that we've ever had. I always took the view that you had to take the rough with the smooth. If you have someone with great talent and ability you have to take some of the drawbacks too.

On Nigel Lawson, BBC TV, 1993

★

He was never popular with the general public who saw what appeared to be a chain-smoking, dishevelled, languid aristocrat; by contrast, he was the object of universal respect and great affection from those who worked with him, above all his officials. Nick had those virtues which seem only to be cultivated in private: he was completely unaffected; he treated people and arguments on their merits; he was incapable of guile; and he was always seeking to take on the unrewarding and unpopular tasks.

On Nicholas Ridley, Downing Street Years, 1993

★

Geoffrey's personal style was very different from mine. He has a lovely speaking voice, a quiet speaking voice. But at Cabinet he always reported on foreign affairs – he always had this quiet voice. It was so quiet sometimes I had to say 'speak up'. And he gave it in a way which wasn't exactly scintillating. And you know, foreign affairs are interesting. They affect everything that happened to our own way of life, and they are exciting. And so we just diverged.

On Sir Geoffrey Howe, BBC TV, 1993

★

In will not take any criticism of Bernard. I could wish that every one of my Ministers had done their job to the same percentage of excellence that Bernard did his.

On Bernard Ingham, BBC TV 1993

★

John is much more a consensus man, and will much more compromise. I had noticed that he tended to go with the crowd and the conventional wisdom, but therefore he needed to be tested to see how he would perform in other roles ... People like John very much, you couldn't not like him. But it's quite different from liking a person, to having a political instinct of the right direction to go in the long run. Perhaps I had developed that over the years.

On John Major, BBC TV, 1993

★

Today I have lost one of my dearest friends, England one of her greatest men. Keith Joseph understood that it was necessary to win again the intellectual argument for freedom, and that to do this we must start from first principles ... He was in many ways an unlikely revolutionary. For all his towering intellect, he was deeply humble. He spoke out boldly, however hostile the audience. Yet he hated to give offence. Above all, his integrity shone out in everything he said and did. His best memorial lies in the younger generations of politicians whom he inspired. But for me he is irreplaceable.

Tribute to Lord Joseph on the day he died, 10 December 1994

On Her Political Opponents

A very good talker, but he is not a doer.
On Harold Wilson, February 1966

★

Some Chancellors are micro-economic. Some Chancellors are fiscal. This one is just plain cheap ... If this Chancellor can be Chancellor, anyone in the House could be Chancellor.
On Denis Healey, January 1975

★

Tony Benn is a skilful politician. He knows when to keep quiet.
1979

★

He presided over debt, drift and decay.
On James Callaghan

★

The SDP MPs should have stayed within the Labour Party
and fought from within it. But they hadn't got the guts.
1 June 1983

★

You would think that his wife would advise him better
wouldn't you?
*On Michael Foot's dress sense, following the Cenotaph service where he wore
a donkey jacket*

★

I could not help feeling sorry for James Callaghan, who
just a little bit earlier had conceded victory in a short
speech, both dignified and generous. Whatever our past
and indeed future disagreements, I believed him to be a
patriot with the interests of Britain at heart, whose worst
tribulations had been inflicted by his own party.
Downing Street Years, 1993

★

The marriage is for one election only. After that either
party can call it a day and go its separate way. Well, of
course, nothing is for ever. But it is an odd couple that
pencils in a date for divorce before they have even sat
down to the wedding breakfast.
*On the SDP/Liberal Alliance, Conservative Party Conference, 16 October
1981*

★

... You belong to the North East, why don't you boost it?
Not always standing there as moaning minnies. Now stop
it!
Description of journalists on Tyneside

★

You don't reach Downing Street by pretending you've
travelled the road to Damascus when you haven't even
left home.
On Neil Kinnock, 1989

★

Little Sir Echo.
On Neil Kinnock, January 1985

★

As for the leaders of the former Alliance parties, I will say
no more than this: they have never learned what every
woman knows – that you can't make a soufflé rise twice.
Conservative Party Conference, 13 October 1989

★

Leading the Labour Party in opposition must be a
nightmare. But I found it difficult to sympathize with Neil
Kinnock. He was involved in what seemed to me a
fundamentally discreditable enterprise, that of making
himself and his party appear what they were not. The
House of Commons and the electorate found him out. As
Opposition Leader he was out of his depth. As Prime
Minister he would have been sunk.
On Neil Kinnock, Downing Street Years, 1993

★

He is probably the most formidable leader we have seen since Gaitskell. I see a lot of Socialism behind their front bench but not in Mr Blair – I think he genuinely has moved.

On Tony Blair, BBC TV, 1994

On Foreign Leaders

He may be a Socialist, but his economic views are more sensible than those of the wets.
On Helmut Schmidt, November 1979

★

It was impossible not to like Jimmy Carter. He was a deeply committed Christian and a man of obvious sincerity. He was also a man of marked intellectual ability and with a grasp, rare among politicians, of science and the scientific method.
On President Carter, Downing Street Years, 1993

★

Charles Haughey was tough, able and politically astute with few illusions and, I am sure, not much affection for the British ... I found him easy to get on with, less talkative and more realistic than Garret Fitzgerald.
Downing Street Years, *1993*

145

★

President Giscard D'Estaing was never someone to whom I warmed. I had the strong impression that the feeling was mutual. This was more surprising than it seems, for I have a soft spot for French charm and, after all, President Giscard was seen as a man of the Right. But he was a difficult interlocutor, speaking in paragraphs of perfectly crafted prose which seemed to brook no interruption.

On President Giscard D'Estaing, Downing Street Years, 1993

★

He seemed to have a positive aversion to principle, even a conviction that a man of principle was doomed to be a figure of fun.

On Guilio Andreotti, Downing Street Years, 1993

★

Pierre, you're being obnoxious. Stop acting like a naughty schoolboy.

On Pierre Trudeau, 1981

★

The election of a man [Ronald Reagan] committed to the cause of freedom and the renewal of America's strength has given encouragement to all those who love liberty.

February 1981

★

I liked and respected Indira Gandhi. Her policies had been more than high-handed, but only a strong figure with a powerful personality could hope successfully to

rule India. Mrs Gandhi was also, perhaps it is not just myth to see this as a female trait – immensely practical. Her weak spot was that she never grasped the importance of the free market.
Downing Street Years, 1993

★

It's a pity about Ronnie [Reagan], he just doesn't understand economics at all.
1983

★

Helmut Schmidt sent nearly half a million Gastarbeiter [immigrant workers] home, which we couldn't do, and he's got compulsory conscription which takes a whole year of young people off the unemployment register. So yes, I get on extremely well with Helmut Schmidt. My policies and his were the same.
BBC Radio, March 1983

★

I like Mr Gorbachev. We can do business together.
On Mikhail Gorbachev, December 1984

★

If you want to cut your own throat, don't come to me for a bandage.
To Robert Mugabe on South African sanctions, July 1986

★

I cannot ever remember having spent so much time with another world leader. If he gave me his word, I would believe him.
On meeting Mikhail Gorbachev in Moscow, April 1987

★

If we let it succeed no small country will feel safe again.
On Iraq's invasion of Kuwait, 2 August 1990

★

All right George, all right. But this is no time to go wobbly.
To George Bush, August 1990

★

This man is a loser ... a person who has taken hostages cruelly, brutally, a person who has hidden behind the' skirts of women and children.
Saddam Hussein, 1990

★

If we cannot visibly support him, then we shall be cheating future generations.
On Mikhail Gorbachev, 1990

★

In the decade of the 80s, Western values were placed in the crucible and they emerged with greater purity and strength. So much of the credit goes to President Reagan. Of him it can be said, as Canning said of Pitt, that he was the pilot that weathered the storm. The world owes him an enormous debt and it saddens me that there are some who refuse to acknowledge his achievements.
Speech to the American Conservative Institutes, 8 March 1991

★

As leader of the Progressive Conservatives I thought he put too much emphasis on the adjective and not enough on the noun.
On former Canadian Prime Minister Brian Mulroney, 1993

★

He would bully me, and I would bully him. Then it was: let's get down to business.
On Mikhail Gorbachev, BBC TV, 1993

★

Your President, President Clinton, is a great communicator. The trouble is, he has absolutely nothing to communicate.
To American political observer, Daniel Forrester, March 1994

★

He does like women, you know.
On François Mitterrand

★

We sometimes seem to be a partnership as indissolubly linked as Astaire and Rogers.
To Ronald Reagan at his 82nd birthday party

The Denouement: Countdown to Midnight

Nigel is a very good Chancellor. Geoffrey is a very good Foreign Secretary – I'm not going any further.
May 1989

★

I do not want you to raise the subject ever again. I must prevail.
To Nigel Lawson on joining the ERM, May 1989

★

I'm making some changes, Geoffrey, and they will involve the Foreign Office.
To Sir Geoffrey Howe, 24 July 1989

★

The Right Team for Britain's Future.
Slogan for the 1989 Conservative Party Conference. Within 13 months five Cabinet Ministers had resigned

★

Advisers advise, Ministers decide.
On her relationship with Sir Alan Walters, 26 October 1989

★

Nigel had determined that he was going to put in his resignation. I did everything possible to stop him.
October 1989

★

Unassailable, unassailable
Description of Nigel Lawson in an interview with Brian Walden, 29 October 1989

★

I'm staying my own sweet reasonable self.
Interview with Brian Walden, 29 October 1989

★

The day Nigel Lawson said 'enough' may be the day that Mrs Thatcher's term of office started to draw to its close.
The Economist, *November 1989*

★

She could so easily have got rid of Walters, but increasingly I fear that she simply cannot bring herself to be on the losing side in any argument. That failing may ditch us all.

William Whitelaw, in a letter to Nigel Lawson following his resignation.

★

By popular acclaim ... let me make it quite clear, I am very happy to carry on.

November 1989

★

I have never been a lame duck in my life and I'm not going to start now. I shall go on as long as I have been elected.

November 1989

★

Mrs Thatcher will find it much harder to win the next election than would another Conservative leader ... her policies are out of tune with the British people ... her European policy is disastrous.

Sir Anthony Meyer, 29 November 1989

★

You are now in danger. This is not a little local difficulty, it's a crisis. Nigel has real standing in the Party and you have rejected his advice, preferring to listen to Alan Walters ... The Party in the House won't like this at all.

Kenneth Baker to Margaret Thatcher following Nigel Lawson's resignation, 26 October 1989

★

I am very pleased with the result. We can now get on with the real issue of tackling inflation. Prime Ministers have a lot of work to do. There is a great pile of it inside and it would be better now if I left you to get on with it.

5 December 1989 following her victory over Sir Anthony Meyer

★

They wanted me to change my style of government, Nick. Why should I change my style of government? I am not going to.

To Nicholas Ridley following a visit from the Executive of the 1922 Committee

★

There are a hundred assassins lurking in the bushes, Prime Minister. Those people will come back and kill you.

Tristan Garel-Jones, following the victory over Sir Anthony Meyer, December 1989

★

Carol Thatcher: Oh well, that's all over then.
Margaret Thatcher: Oh no, that's just the beginning

Following the victory over Sir Anthony Meyer, December 1989

The Denouement:
Let Battle Commence

History may tell how much Ian [Gow] did to lubricate the relationship between PM and Chancellor between 1979 and 1983. It was in the highest tradition of Wykehamist subtlety.

Peter Cropper, former Special Adviser to Sir Geoffrey Howe, 1990

★

I'm still at the crease, though the bowling's been pretty hostile of late. And, in case anyone doubted it, can I assure you that there will be no ducking the bouncers, no stonewalling, no playing for time? The bowling's going to get hit all round the ground. That's my style.

Lord Mayor's Banquet, 12 November 1990

★

154

I believe both the Chancellor and the Governor are cricketing enthusiasts so I hope there will be no monopoly of cricketing metaphors. It's rather like sending your opening batsmen to the crease only for them to find that before the first ball is bowled, their bats have been broken by the team captain ... The time has come for others to consider their own response to the tragic conflict of loyalties with which I have myself wrestled for perhaps too long.

Sir Geoffrey Howe, resignation speech to the House of Commons, 13 November 1990

★

Mrs Thatcher started with a look of tense composure and a faint smile. The composure held, the tension grew, and the smile disappeared.

Matthew Parris, describing in The Times, *Mrs Thatcher's appearance during Sir Geoffrey Howe's resignation speech, 13 November 1990*

★

I was just amazed by the mixture of bile and treachery which just poured out. In a speech, every word of which had clearly been carefully drafted and in a speech, which he delivered, if I might say so, better than any speech I had ever heard him deliver. Perhaps this was his feelings coming to the fore ... I had to sit with my back to him [Geoffrey Howe]. I could have turned round to see him but I didn't particularly wish to. I knew the press were facing me in the gallery opposite me so I knew I must keep my features composed and calm. At the same time I was trying to assess the effect that speech would have because I knew some of the rumours and discussions which were taking place. It is an experience I would not

wish to repeat ... In the end it was not my record which he assassinated. He assassinated his own character.
BBC TV, 1993

★

Mrs Thatcher has been bitten by the man she treated as a doormat – and she deserves it.
Neil Kinnock, 13 November 1990

★

She must go on.
John Major, 13 November 1990

★

I am persuaded that I now have a better prospect than Mrs Thatcher of leading the Conservatives to a fourth electoral victory and preventing the calamity of a Labour Government.
Michael Heseltine, 14 November 1990

★

In truth, it is difficult to run a campaign without the presence of the candidate.
Sir Norman Fowler

★

After three general election victories, leading the only Party with clear policies resolutely carried out, I intend to continue.
15 November 1990

★

Journalist: Under no circumstances would you stand?
Douglas Hurd: Against her.
16 November 1990

★

As proposer and seconder of the Prime Minister in the leadership election we both want to make it quite clear that what we wish to see is a good victory for Mrs Thatcher in the first and only ballot.
Statement by Douglas Hurd and John Major, 17 November 1990

★

Mrs Thatcher deserves better than to be dismissed in the shoddy and demeaning manner some Tory MPs are minded to have in store for her.
Peregrine Worsthorne in the Sunday Telegraph, *18 November 1990*

★

If we win according to the rules, we win. The rules were not made by me. I abide by the rules. I expect others to abide by the rules.
Margaret Thatcher in an interview with the Sunday Telegraph, *18 November 1990*

★

We lost everything because we had gone too far to the left. We had strayed from every single thing we believed in. If you read Michael Heseltine's book, you will find it more akin to some of the Labour Party policies: intervention, corporatism, everything that pulled us

down. There is a fundamental difference on economics and there's no point trying to hide it. Those of us who sat with Michael on economic discussions remember full well.
Margaret Thatcher in an interview with The Times, *19 November 1990*

★

Not, I'm afraid, as good as we had hoped.
Peter Morrison, about to give the results of the leadership election to Mrs Thatcher, 1990

★

Prime Minister, it's here, this is the microphone.
BBC Political Correspondent, John Serjeant, outside the Paris Embassy, November 1990

★

I'm naturally very pleased that I got more than half the parliamentary party and disappointed that it's not enough to win on the first ballot so I confirm it is my intention to let my name go forward for the second ballot.
Outside the Paris Embassy, November 1990

★

The Prime Minister continues to have my full support and I am sorry this destructive, unnecessary contest should be prolonged in this way.
Douglas Hurd, outside the Paris Embassy, November 1990

The Denouement:
The Final Hours

I fight on, I fight to win.
Upon leaving Downing Street for the Commons, 21 November 1990

★

Now look here, you miserable little worm. You are in this
Cabinet because I put you there and for no other reason.
So I expect your support, and if I don't get it you will be
out of my Cabinet when I reshuffle it after all this
nonsense is over.
*Cecil Parkinson outlining what he thought Margaret Thatcher should have
said to errant Ministers*

★

I was sick at heart. I could have resisted the opposition of
opponents and potential rivals and even respected them
for it; but what grieved me was the desertion of those I

had always considered friends and allies and the weasel words whereby they had transmuted their betrayal into frank advice and concern for my fate.
Downing Street Years, *1993*

★

It was treachery with a smile on his face. Perhaps that was the worst thing of all.
Describing her betrayal by the Cabinet, BBC TV, 1993

★

Margaret Thatcher: Will you please second my nomination?
[Long pause]
John Major: If that's what you want me to do, I'll do it.

★

She may lose but she might win but if she's going to go down, she must go down fighting.
Alan Clark, 21 November 1990

★

The fight is over. The battle is lost. You should withdraw from the field.
Kenneth Clarke, 21 November 1990

★

Fuck the typing George, let's go and see her.
David Maclean to Sir George Gardiner, 21 November 1990

★

We've come to bully you, Margaret.
Sir George Gardiner, in a vain attempt to persuade Mrs Thatcher to contest the second round of the leadership contest, 21 November 1990.

★

Alan Clark: You're in a jam.
Margaret Thatcher: I know that.
AC: They're all telling you not to stand aren't they?
MT: I'm going to stand. I have issued a statement.
AC: That's wonderful. That's heroic. But the Party will let you down.
MT: I am a fighter.
AC: Fight then. Fight right to the end, a third ballot if you need to, but you lose.
MT: It'd be so terrible if Michael won. He would undo everything I have fought for.
AC: But what a way to go! Unbeaten in three elections, never rejected by the people. Brought down by nonentities!
MT: But Michael ... as Prime Minister!
AC: Who the fuck's Michael? No one. Nothing. He won't last six months. I doubt if he'd even win the election. Your place in history is towering ...MT: Alan, it's been so good of you to come in and see me.
From Alan Clark's Diaries

★

Darling, I don't want you to be humiliated.
Denis Thatcher, 21 November 1990

★

It would have saved us an awful lot of bother if she had got four more votes.
Norman Tebbit

The Denouement: Resignation

Margaret Thatcher: Having consulted widely among colleagues ... [breaks down, wiping tears from her eyes] ... I am so sorry ...
Cecil Parkinson: For God's sake, you read it, James.
Margaret Thatcher: [blows her nose] I have concluded that the unity of the Party and the prospects of victory in the general election [breaks down again] ... will be better served if I stood down to enable Cabinet colleagues to enter the ballot for the leadership. I should like to thank all those in Cabinet and outside who have given me such dedicated support. It is vital that we stand together. The unity of the Party is crucial and that's why I'm giving up. I couldn't bear all the things I have stood for over the past eleven years being rejected. The Cabinet must unite to stop Michael Heseltine.

Resignation statement to the Cabinet, 22 November 1990

★

You have and will always continue to have the love and loyalty of the Party. You have a special place in the heart of the Party. You have led us to victory three times and you would have done so again. Those who have served you realize that they have been in touch with greatness.
Kenneth Baker at the Cabinet meeting, 22 November 1990

★

This is a typically brave and selfless decision by the Prime Minister. Once again Margaret Thatcher has put her country and the Party's interests before personal considerations. This will allow the Party to elect a new leader to unite the Party and build upon her immense success. If I could just add a personal note, I am very saddened that our greatest peace-time Prime Minister has left government. She is an outstanding leader, not only of our country, but also of the world. I do not believe we will see her like again.
Kenneth Baker to reporters outside 10 Downing Street following the Cabinet meeting, 22 November 1990

★

Rejoice, Rejoice!
Edward Heath, November 1990

★

The Labour Party is led by a pygmy and we are led by a giant. We have decided that the answer to our problems is to find a pygmy of our own.
Cecil Parkinson, November 1990

The Denouement:
I'm Enjoying This

Mr Kinnock, in all his years as Opposition Leader, never let me down. On this occasion he delivered a speech that might have served if I had announced my intention to stand for the second ballot. It was a standard, partisan rant ... He managed to fill me and the benches behind me with his own partisan indignation and therefore intensified the newfound Tory unity – in the circumstances a remarkable, if perverse achievement.

On Neil Kinnock's speech in the no confidence debate, Downing Street Years, *1993*

★

Margaret Thatcher: Europe is strongest when it grows through willing co-operation and practical measures, not compulsion or bureaucratic dreams.
Alan Beith: Will the Prime Minister tell us whether she

intends to continue her personal fight against a single currency and an independent central bank when she leaves office?

Dennis Skinner: No, she's going to be the governor (*laughter*)

Margaret Thatcher: What a good idea! I hadn't thought of that. But if I were, there'd be no European central bank, accountable to no one, not least of all to national Parliaments. Because the point of that kind of Europe with a central bank is no democracy, taking powers away from every single Parliament, and having a single currency, monetary policy and interest rates, which takes all political power away from us. As my Right Honourable Friend [Nigel Lawson] said in his first speech after the proposal for a single currency, a single currency is about the politics of Europe. It is about a federal Europe by the back door. So I'll consider the Honourable Gentleman's [Mr Skinner's] proposal. Now, where were we? I'm enjoying this, I'm enjoying this!

Michael Carttiss: Cancel it. You can wipe the floor with these people!

Hansard, *no confidence debate, 22 November, 1990*

★

Twice in my time as Prime Minister we have had to send our forces across the world to defend a small country against ruthless aggression: first to our own people in the Falklands and now to the borders of Kuwait. To those who have never had to take such decisions, I say that they are taken with a heavy heart and in the knowledge of the manifold dangers, but with tremendous pride in the professionalism and courage of our armed forces. There is something else which one feels. That is a sense of the country's destiny: the centuries of history and experience which ensure that, when principles have to be defended, when good has to be upheld and when evil has to be overcome, Britain will take up arms. It is because we on this side have never flinched from difficult decisions that this House and this country can have confidence in this Government.

Hansard, *her final words in the no confidence debate, 22 November 1990*

★

It is impossible to follow the Prime Minister without soberly reflecting for a moment that we have heard what is probably the last of her important and considerable speeches from the Government dispatch box. It was a bravura performance of the sort which she has made her own. I cannot with honesty say I shall miss it, but I shall certainly remember it and, as time intervenes, remember it with ever greater affection ... It is impossible to have lived through last week without feeling that one is participating in a moment of history.

Paddy Ashdown, following Margaret Thatcher in the no confidence debate, 22 November 1990

★

What she was doing was casting off all restraint and really shouting the things she had always wanted to shout but which people had advised her not to.

Edward Heath, Independent on Sunday, *23 January 1990*

★

We had a fantastic time. When it came to answering the Motion of No Confidence I felt it was no holds barred. I had beaten these people hollow for years and I thought now let me have one last go and we did. It was quite a go.

Interview with Barbara Walters, February 1991

Life After
Downing Street

Now it is time for a new chapter to begin and I wish John Major all the luck in the world.

On the steps of 10 Downing Street as she left it for the last time, 27 November 1990

★

It's a funny old world.

At a Cabinet meeting following her resignation, 27 November 1990

★

The same person in a slightly different capacity will be available to serve Great Britain in whatever way it happens.

22 November 1990

★

That thing in November.
The phrase Lady Thatcher is reputed to use when referring to the leadership election and her resignation

★

It is the move I would have least wanted to do.
Michael Gersman, head of the removal company which moved the Thatchers from Downing Street to Dulwich

★

I shan't be pulling the levers, but I shall be a very good back-seat driver.
On her role following her departure from Number Ten, 1990

★

I have done pretty well out of being Mrs Thatcher.
On what she should be called following the award of a Baronetcy to Denis Thatcher

★

She will need people close to her, to help her and to wipe the tears, because there will be some, whether real or metaphorical.
Professor Cary Cooper

★

You told me that I would have had to do something about the Community Charge. I would have found that difficult. You also told me that I would have had to ring up MPs

and spend my time in the tea room. That's not for me after eleven years.
To Kenneth Baker a week after her resignation

★

I wouldn't change any of my policies if I had my time again, and no, no, no, I don't spend my time regretting.
Independent on Sunday, *16 January 1990*

★

Sometimes I say, 'Which day is it?' I never said that at Number Ten.
11 May 1991

★

Home is where you come to when you've nothing better to do.
11 May 1991

★

I can defend it clearly, explicitly at any time, in any place and to any person.
On the Community Charge (Poll Tax), 8 June 1991

★

I've been very quiet at home, which has been a very great effort on my part. A little less silence might be called for on my part.
Speaking about Europe, 22 June 1991

★

I shall go on doing things until I march up to the Pearly Gates and say, I've come – have you got any work for me yet?
Independent, 6 July 1991

★

The worst thing is the realization that some of those who you most trusted were most prominent in your betrayal.
Speaking after the coup against Mikhail Gorbachev, 31 August 1991

★

I found that she was not at all bitter. She was really rather stunned. She couldn't quite believe it had happened and she couldn't quite understand how it had happened. But she is a very practical person and she had to get on with the business of organizing her life.
Cecil Parkinson, World in Action, *11 November 1991*

★

At times she suddenly seemed to lose focus. It was like seeing a dear friend under sedation.
Lord Gowrie, 1991

★

It's a traumatic shock, it really is. You don't realize until you're out. Even now when we're driving down Whitehall my mind still thinks we'll turn right into Downing Street, then I realize we're not going to. And then you realize it's not you any more.
Interview with Barbara Walters, February 1991

★

I see a tendency to try to undermine what I achieved and to go back to more powers for government. That would be totally wrong for a proud and free people.

Interview with Barbara Walters, February 1991

★

I think it is wrong to have a contest for the leadership while you're Prime Minister. I am the first Conservative Prime Minister who has been subject to that. I don't think it does any good for the office of Prime Minister. I hope they'll never have it again. I think it is wrong.

Interview with Barbara Walters, February 1991

★

I have never been defeated by the people. It is my great pride.

Interview with Barbara Walters, February 1991

★

It is my purpose to continue to be a strong ally and friend of Prime Minister Major and the Government he leads.

After announcing she would stand down at the 1992 General Election, June 1991

★

The enjoyment of the backbenches comes from being able to speak out freely. This, however, I knew would never again be possible. My every word would be judged in terms of support for or opposition to John Major. I would inhibit him just by my presence, and that in turn would inhibit me.

On her decision not to stand in the 1992 General Election, Path to Power, *1995*

★

John Major is doing wonders.
Interview with Barbara Walters, February 1992

★

It's quite a wrench. I shan't realize it fully until after the election night and after the assembly of Parliament.
On standing down as MP for Finchley, 28 March 1992

★

I think Essex Man will vote for a Conservative Government.
During general election campaign, 4 April 1992

★

I do not accept the idea that all of a sudden Major is now his own man. There isn't any such thing as Majorism.
25 April 1992

★

It's very nervy. It's such a hot day, too hot to be wearing such heavy clothes.
Upon taking her seat in the House of Lords, 30 June 1992

★

It is a privilege to take my place on these distinguished, tranquil benches after 33 years before the mast in another place.
Her first words to the House of Lords, 2 July 1992

★

I calculate that I was responsible for proposing the elevation to the Lords of some 214 of its present numbers.
House of Lords, 2 July 1992

★

I have never knowingly made a non-controversial speech in my life.
2 July 1992

★

I never felt the need for a virility symbol.
On the eve of the French referendum on the Maastricht Treaty, 26 September 1992

★

I was sick at heart. I could have resisted the opposition of opponents and potential rivals and even respected them for it; but what grieved me was the desertion of those I had always considered friends and allies and the weasel words whereby they had transmuted their betrayal into frank advice and concern for my fate.
Downing Street Years, 1993

★

I have been in Parliament for 34 years. I cannot remember a time when politicians were so out of touch with the people and so in touch with each other.
18 April 1993

★

You can't lead an 'if only' life. There's always a future, there's always work. I shall work till my dying day.
23 October 1993

★

Life is a choice of alternatives and in my view John is the best of the three.
BBC Radio 2, 24 October 1993

★

I understand now that those marvellous working miners, the Democratic Union, feel a sense of betrayal.
On the Government's pit closure plans, 30 October 1993

★

I've just had the honour of delivering the speech at Ronald Reagan's 84th birthday celebrations. I'm only 69. Just the age Ronald was when he became President, and I must say I'm feeling a little underemployed.
7 February 1995

★

They have hit at everything I believed in.
On the Major Government, 12 June 1995

★

Insofar as we are down in the opinion polls it is because we have not been Conservative enough.
17 June 1995

★

I don't think I was unkind to him. I supported him a lot – I chose him!
Referring to John Major, 23 June 1995

★

I cannot leave the future alone. I don't want it to go wonky or wobbly.
24 June 1995

★

In Britain, we're all Thatcherites now.
At a party in the United States given in honour of her 70th birthday, 24 October 1995

★

Get cracking.
Urging Conservatives to support John Major, 9 October 1996

★

I am so pleased that after four election defeats they have now come to terms with the 1980s. Perhaps after four more they will come to terms with the 1990s. I am told we are all Thatcherites now. My goodness me, never has the road to Damascus been so congested.
Daily Telegraph, *9 December 1996*

Tributes

When she came to power in 1979 we genuinely debated whether or not those who governed Britain would be the trade unions or the elected government of our country. I think her most significant achievement is that that question is no longer asked. She has had a unique character and unique strengths and abilities and unique faults as well.

Paddy Ashdown, BBC TV News, 22 November 1990

★

May I pay tribute to you on your decision this morning. You showed by that that you amount to more than those who have turned against you in recent days.

Neil Kinnock at Prime Minister's Questions, 22 November 1990

★

She had a profound influence on President Reagan and particularly in his approach to what he had characterized as the evil empire. Five years later, if Margaret Thatcher, his close colleague and philosophical soulmate, is saying, look, we can do business with this guy, that's very persuasive to President Reagan, I think. In fact, I know it was because I was there.

James Baker, BBC TV, 1993

★

I think Mrs Thatcher did more damage to democracy, equality, internationalism, civil liberties, freedom in this country than any other Prime Minister this century. When the euphoria surrounding her departure subsides you will find that in a year or two's time there will not be a Tory who admits ever supporting her. People in the streets will say, thank God she's gone.

Tony Benn, The Thatcher Factor, *Channel 4, December 1990*

★

It was a surprise. In our imagination she was the Iron Lady who would fight to the end. She was a historic figure who helped bring the Soviet Union closer to Europe.

Gennadi Gerasimov, Soviet Foreign Ministry spokesman, 22 November 1990

★

I'll miss her because I value her counsel. I value her long experience and the wisdom that comes from that experience. She has been an outstanding Prime Minister for the United Kingdom and an outstanding friend to the United States.

President George Bush, 22 November 1990

★

Margaret Thatcher was the hardest-working head of Government I ever met. Her application was prodigious and she was always extraordinarily well briefed for every meeting. Whatever the subject, she could press her sometimes jarring and belligerent viewpoints with great authority, and for that I deeply respected her.

Bob Hawke, Australian Prime Minister 1983–91

★

She has made a remarkable contribution to Britain's history and has led this country with great distinction in the 1980s.

Michael Heseltine, BBC TV News, 22 November 1990

★

The Iron Lady was a great lady. She deserves applause.

Valery Giscard D'Estaing, 22 November 1990

★

I think we were all shocked, and the President [Jacques Delors] immediately said his overwhelming feeling was of one of the highest esteem of the Prime Minister despite the differences and disagreements.

Sir Leon Brittan, 22 November 1990

★

Margaret Thatcher was beyond argument a great Prime Minister. Her tragedy is that she may be remembered less for the brilliance of her many achievements than for the recklessness with which she later sought to impose her own increasingly uncompromising views.

Sir Geoffrey Howe, 1994

★

It is quite clear that history will record that Margaret Thatcher was the greatest Prime Minister this country has had since Churchill.

Nigel Lawson, The Times, 23 November 1990

★

I should like to thank you for the great co-operation and friendship which you have shown me during our time together in office during which so much has been achieved.

Charles Haughey, Irish Prime Minister, in a letter, November 1990

★

You are always welcome in Czechoslovakia.

Vaclav Havel

★

So long Maggie, we want you to know
We still love you, even though you must go
We'll all miss you, when you leave Number Ten
So farewell Maggie, but come back again
They say a week in politics
Can be a long wait
But you stayed on eleven years
And made Great Britain great

Max Bygraves, LBC Newstalk, 26 November 1990

★

You have done more than any of us ever thought possible and ever hoped to do. You were a great leader, a giant – a beautiful giant.

Sir Keith Joseph, 26 November 1990

*

She has been a strong and courageous Prime Minister, always sustained by her Christian faith. I pray that her experience and gifts may continue to be at the service of the nation.

Archbishop of Canterbury, Dr Robert Runcie, The Times, *23 November 1990*

*

Mrs Thatcher will be remembered not as a great executive leader, because every Prime Minister is powerful, but because she is a teacher. The weakness of the Labour Party over a long period is that it hasn't done any teaching.

Tony Benn, 8 February 1992

*

I should like to offer my heartfelt tribute, on behalf of so very many, to our fine leader of yore, on the day, remembered throughout the world, when a much revered lady stood down, apparently at the request of her Party, with dignity and grace.

Judith Gardner from Oxford, in a letter to the Sunday Telegraph, *22 November 1992*

*

You are the only person so far to whom has been awarded the Order of the Handbag.

George Schultz to Margaret Thatcher at his farewell party, December 1992

★

She's the Prime Minister who really wanted to be Queen. Major's boring, the Prime Minister who wanted to be a train spotter.
Thatcher impersonator, Steve Nallon, BBC TV 1993

★

My admiration for Mrs Thatcher is extremely high. She is imposing and articulate, an ideological politician instead of a compromiser. She was a great Prime Minister and her influence was felt around the world.
Vice President Dan Quayle, 1994

★

The nation was oppressed by many dragons in 1979. Margaret Thatcher came forth to slay them. After she had slain them the nation no longer had need of her. Normal, humdrum government has been resumed. We shall miss her style of government.
Nicholas Ridley, 1991

★

Her influence was very constructive, so I was always glad to see her coming. As a matter of fact sometimes when I was trying to persuade the President of something that I knew she agreed with but he was reluctant about I was shameless in saying, Mr President, here's what Margaret Thatcher says on that subject. She's looked into it, so hear me out on this.
George Schultz, BBC TV, 1993

★

I think her greatest achievement is to have made people believe that the impossible is possible. That the things which were said in 1979 to be beyond resolution, the problem of the trade unions for example, she boldly took it on and she did it. If politicians can learn that lesson from her, that there is no problem which is too big to be solved, then she's contributed something enormously important to our life.

Norman Tebbit, The Thatcher Factor, *Channel 4, December 1990*

★

A rare leader who had strong beliefs and revitalized the United Kingdom.

Toshiki Kaifu, Japanese Prime Minister, 22 November 1990

★

I think the rest of the world will think we're mad, and indeed we are. We've turned out the greatest Prime Minister in the post-war years simply because of short-term nerves.

Ann Widdecombe, BBC TV News, 22 November 1990

★

We have lost a leader who shared our views and for whom we had tremendous admiration, love and respect.

Nicholas Bennett, a member of the Thatcherite No Turning Back group of MPs, 22 November 1990

★

We would find it rather difficult to do that.

German Government spokesman when asked for a tribute to Margaret Thatcher, 22 November 1990

★

I am horrified, I am disgusted with the Tory Party. I think it is tantamount to committing political suicide that we have put on one side and forced to resign, the greatest political leader in the United Kingdom this century.
Nicholas Winterton MP, BBC TV News, 22 November 1990

★

A remarkable lady, an extraordinary personality who I am sure will go down in history as one of the more significant British Prime Ministers.
Henry Kissinger, 22 November 1990

★

The gentlemen in grey suits should now be visited by gentlemen in white coats.
Letter to The Times, *23 November 1990*

★

We do not have to like our political leaders; we must respect them. Margaret Thatcher can never be accused of courting popularity; nobody, however, commands more respect in rank and file Tories at home or amongst other world leaders. It is a tragedy for Britain that she has decided to resign.
Letter to The Times, *26 November 1990*

★

A lady sent to us on wings from heaven.
Rocco Forte

★

She was a tigress surrounded by hamsters.
John Biffen, Observer, *December 1990*

★

The further you got from Britain, the more admired you found she was.
James Callaghan, The Spectator, *December 1990*

★

The greatest Briton since Winston Churchill.
Charles Price, 1991

The Top Ten

It will be years, and not in my time, before a woman will
lead the Party or become Prime Minister.
1974

★

No! No! No!
Opposing proposals put forward by Jacques Delors, 1990

★

Where there is discord may we bring harmony. Where
there is error, may we bring truth. Where there is doubt,
may we bring faith. Where there is despair, may we bring
hope.
Quoting St Francis of Assisi on the steps of 10 Downing Street, May 1979

★

To those waiting with baited breath for that favourite media catchphrase, the U Turn, I have only one thing to say. You turn if you want to. The Lady's not for turning.
Conservative Party Conference, 10 October 1980

★

Just rejoice at the news and congratulate our armed forces and the Marines. Rejoice!
To journalists, following the retaking of South Georgia, 1982

★

There is no such thing as Society. There are individual men and women, and there are families.
1987

★

It was treachery with a smile on its face. Perhaps that was the worst thing of all.
Describing her betrayal by the Cabinet, BBC TV, 1993

★

Is he one of us?
Phrase coined to describe those of Thatcherite views

★

The enemy within.
Describing militant mineworkers to the 1922 Committee, 19 July 1984

★

We have become a Grandmother.
To reporters outside 10 Downing Street, 1989

Maggie's Ministers

In her eleven and a half years in power 60 Ministers served in Mrs Thatcher's Cabinet – of them, only one was a woman.

Humphrey Atkins   1979–82   Resigned (Falklands)
Kenneth Baker   1985–90   Final Cabinet
Lord Belstead   1987–90   Final Cabinet
John Biffen   1979–87   Sacked
Leon Brittan   1981–86   Resigned (Westland)
Peter Brooke   1987–90   Final Cabinet
Mark Carlisle   1979–81   Sacked
Lord Carrington   1979–82   Resigned (Falklands)
Paul Channon   1986–89   Sacked
Kenneth Clarke   1985–90   Final Cabinet
Lord Cockfield   1982–84   Sacked
Nicholas Edwards   1979–87   Sacked
Norman Fowler   1981–90   Resigned (Personal reasons)
Sir Ian Gilmour   1979–81   Sacked
Earl of Gowrie   1984–85   Resigned (Financial reasons)

John Gummer   1989–90   Final Cabinet
Lord Hailsham   1979–87   Sacked
Sir Michael Havers   1979–87   Sacked
Michael Heseltine   1979–86   Resigned (Westland)
Michael Howard   1990   Final Cabinet
Sir Geoffrey Howe   1979–90   Resigned (Europe)
David Howell   1979–81   Sacked
David Hunt   1990   Final Cabinet
Douglas Hurd   1984–90   Final Cabinet
Patrick Jenkin   1979–85   Sacked
Michael Jopling   1979–87   Sacked
Sir Keith Joseph   1979–86   Resigned (Personal reasons)
Tom King   1983–90   Final Cabinet
Norman Lamont   1989–90   Final Cabinet
Nigel Lawson   1981–89   Resigned (Economic Policy)
Peter Lilley   1990   Final Cabinet
Lord MacKay of Clashfern   1987–90   Final Cabinet
John MacGregor   1985–90   Final Cabinet
John Major   1987–90   Final Cabinet
Angus Maude   1979–81   Sacked
Sir Patrick Mayhew   1987–90   Final Cabinet
John Moore   1986–89   Sacked
Tony Newton   1988–90   Final Cabinet
John Nott   1979–83   Resigned (Personal reasons)
Cecil Parkinson   1979–83, 87–90   Final Cabinet
Christopher Patten   1989–90   Final Cabinet
James Prior   1979–84   Sacked
Francis Pym   1979–83   Sacked
Peter Rees   1983–85   Sacked
Tim Renton   1989–90   Final Cabinet
Nicholas   Ridley   1981–90   Resigned   (Anti-German comments)
Malcolm Rifkind   1986–90   Final Cabinet
Lord Soames   1979–81   Sacked
Norman St John Stevas   1979–81   Sacked
Norman Tebbit   1981–87   Resigned (Personal reasons)

David Waddington   1987–90   Final Cabinet
John Wakeham   1983–90   Final Cabinet
William Waldegrave   1990   Final Cabinet
Peter Walker   1979–90   Resigned (Personal reasons)
William Whitelaw   1979–88   Resigned (Health)
Lady Young   1982–83   Sacked
Lord Young   1984–89   Resigned (Personal reasons)
George Younger   1979–89   Resigned (Personal reasons)

Career Chronology

13 October 1925	Born in Grantham
23 February 1950	Fights Dartford constituency at General Election
25 October 1951	Fights Dartford constituency at General Election
8 October 1959	Wins Finchley constituency at General Election
5 February 1960	Makes maiden speech in the House of Commons
February–October 1960	Parliamentary passage of MT's Public Bodies (Admission of the Press to Meetings) Bill
9 October 1961	Appointed Parliamentary Secretary at the Ministry for Pensions and National Insurance in Harold Macmillan's Government
28 October 1964	Appointed Opposition Spokesman on Pensions

5 October 1965	Appointed Shadow Spokesman for Housing and Land
19 April 1966	Appointed as Shadow Treasury Spokesman under Iain Macleod
12 October 1966	Makes first speech from the platform at the Conservative Party Conference
10 October 1967	Appointed to the Shadow Cabinet as Shadow Spokesman on Fuel and Power
10 October 1968	Gives annual *Conservative Political Centre* lecture on 'What's wrong with politics'.
14 November 1968	Appointed Shadow Transport Spokesman
21 November 1969	Appointed Shadow Education Spokesman
19 June 1970	Appointed Secretary of State for Education in Edward Heath's Cabinet
May 1974	Forms *Centre for Policy Studies* think tank with Sir Keith Joseph
4 February 1975	Defeats Edward Heath in first round of Conservative Party leadership election
11 February 1975	Elected leader of the Conservative Party
28 March 1979	Labour Government is defeated on a motion of no confidence
3 May 1979	Leads Conservative Party to general election victory with a majority of 43
12 June 1979	Budget cuts standard rate of income tax from 33p to 30p but VAT is nearly doubled to 15 per cent
5 May 1980	Orders SAS to storm Iranian embassy after terrorist siege
5 January 1981	First reshuffle involves sacking of Norman St John Stevas
1 March 1981	Refuses to bow to IRA hunger strikers' demands for political status
14 September 1981	Second Cabinet reshuffle sees sacking

	of Ian Gilmour and Christopher Soames and promotion of Nigel Lawson, Cecil Parkinson and Norman Tebbit. Jim Prior moved to Northern Ireland from Employment
2 April 1982	Argentina invades the Falkland Islands
2 May 1982	Gives Task Force permission to sink Argentinian battlecruiser *General Belgrano*
14 June 1982	British forces capture Port Stanley ending the Falklands War
9 June 1983	Leads Conservative Party to second General Election victory with a record majority of 144
11 June 1983	Reshuffles Cabinet. Nigel Lawson becomes Chancellor, Leon Brittan becomes Home Secretary and Sir Geoffrey Howe goes to the Foreign Office
25 October 1983	Condemns US invasion of Grenada
22 April 1984	Breaks off diplomatic relations with Libya over shooting of WPC Yvonne Fletcher outside Libyan Embassy
12 October 1984	IRA bomb explodes in Brighton hotel yards from Margaret Thatcher's room
15 December 1984	First meeting with Mikhail Gorbachev at Chequers
19 December 1984	Signs agreement with China transferring Hong Kong to China in 1997
20 February 1985	Addresses both Houses of the US Congress
3 March 1985	National Union of Mineworkers calls off year long coal strike
5 September 1985	Cabinet reshuffle sees Douglas Hurd, John MacGregor, Kenneth Clarke and Kenneth Baker join the Cabinet

15 November 1985 Signs Anglo-Irish Agreement
9 January 1986   Defence Secretary Michael Heseltine
                     resigns from the Cabinet over the West-
                     land affair
17 February 1986   Signs the Single European Act
15 April 1986   Allows US bombers to fly from Britain
                     to bomb Libyan targets
11 June 1987   Leads Conservative Party to third
                     General Election victory with a majority
                     of 101
15 March 1988   Budget cuts basic rate of tax to 25p and
                     the top rate to 40p
20 September 1988 Makes controversial speech in Bruges
                     on the future of Europe
26 June 1989   Nigel Lawson and Sir Geoffrey Howe
                     secretly threaten to resign if MT does
                     not agree to their policy on joining the
                     Exchange Rate Mechanism
24 July 1989   Cabinet reshuffle demotes Sir Geoffrey
                     Howe. John Major becomes Foreign
                     Secretary
26 October 1989   Nigel Lawson resigns as Chancellor.
                     John Major takes over
5 December 1989   Wins Conservative Party leadership
                     contest by 314 to Sir Anthony Meyer's
                     33 votes with 27 abstentions
14 July 1990   Key Cabinet ally Nicholas Ridley
                     resigns following anti-German
                     comments
30 July 1990   Another ally, former PPS Ian Gow, is
                     killed by an IRA car bomb
2 August 1990   Iraq invades Kuwait. MT is with George
                     Bush in Aspen
3 October 1990   Bows to pressure from Chancellor John
                     Major to enter the ERM
27 October 1990   Special EC summit in Rome prompts

	'No, No, No' to a single currency
1 November 1990	Sir Geoffrey Howe resigns from the Cabinet
22 November 1990	Resignation as Conservative Party leader
28 November 1990	Last day as Prime Minister
June 1991	Announces she will stand down as an MP at the next General Election
9 April 1992	Stands down as Member of Parliament for Finchley
30 June 1992	Takes her seat in the House of Lords as Baroness Thatcher of Kesteven
2 July 1992	Makes her maiden speech in the House of Lords
October 1993	First volume of memoirs, *The Downing Street Years*, is published
October 1995	Second volume of memoirs, *The Path to Power*, is published

Select Bibliography

Baker, Kenneth, *The Turbulent Years – My Life in Politics* (Faber and Faber, 1993)

Clark, Alan, *Diaries* (Weidenfeld and Nicolson, 1994)

Collins, Ian, *Westminster Exposed* (Jarrold, 1988)

Day, Sir Robin, *Grand Inquisitor* (Weidenfeld and Nicolson, 1989)

Gove, Michael, *Michael Portillo – Future of the Right* (Fourth Estate, 1995)

Green, Jonathon, *Book of Political Quotes* (Angus and Robertson, 1982)

Harris, Robert, *Good and Faithful Servant* (Faber and Faber, 1990)

Hawke, Bob, *The Hawke Memoirs* (Heinemann, 1994)

Henderson, Sir Nicholas, *Mandarin* (Weidenfeld and Nicolson, 1994)

Henning, Chuck, *Wit and Wisdom of Politics* (Fulcrum, 1992)

Howe, Sir Geoffrey, *Conflict of Loyalty* (Macmillan, 1994)

Ingham, Bernard, *Kill the Messenger* (HarperCollins, 1993)

Jarman, Colin, *Guinness Dictionary of Poisonous Quotes* (Guinness, 1991)

Jenkins, Roy, *A Life at the Centre* (Macmillan, 1991)

Jones, Graham, *Forked Tongues* (Century, 1984)

Jones, Graham, *Forked Tongues Annual* (Century, 1985)

Jones, Graham, *Official Candidate's Book of Political Insults* (Century, 1987)

Junor, Sir John, *Listening for a Midnight Tram* (Chapmans, 1990)

Knight, Greg, *Honourable Insults* (Robson Books, 1990)

Knight, Greg, *Parliamentary Sauce* (Robson Books, 1993)

Lawson, Nigel, *The View from Number 11* (Bantam, 1992)

McFadyean, Melanie, *Thatcher's Reign – A Bad Case of the Blues* (Chatto and Windus, 1984)

Millar, Ronald, *A View from the Wings* (Weidenfeld and Nicolson, 1993)

Parkinson, Cecil, *Right at the Centre* (Weidenfeld and Nicolson, 1992)

Parris, Matthew and Mason, Phil, *Read my Lips* (Robson Books, 1996)

Prior, James, *Balance of Power* (Hamish Hamilton, 1986)

Ranelagh, John, *Thatcher's People* (HarperCollins, 1991)

Ridley, Nicholas, *My Style of Government* (Century, 1991)

Rogers, Michael, *Political Quotes* (Sphere, 1982)

Smith, Geoffrey, *Reagan and Thatcher* (Bodley Head, 1990)

Thatcher, Carol, *Diary of an Election* (Sidgwick and Jackson, 1983)

Thatcher, Carol, *Below the Parapet* (HarperCollins, 1996)

Thatcher, Margaret, *Speeches to the Conservative Party Conference 1975-88* (CPC, 1989)

Thatcher, Margaret, *The Downing Street Years* (HarperCollins, 1993)

Thatcher, Margaret, *The Path to Power* (HarperCollins, 1995)

Tomlinson, Gerald, *Speaker's Treasury of Political Stories, Anecdotes and Humour* (MJF, 1990)

Urban, George, *Diplomacy and Disillusion* (I B Tauris, 1996)

Watkins, Alan, *A Conservative Coup* (Duckworth, 1991)

Young, Hugo, *The Thatcher Phenomenon* (BBC Books, 1985)

Biographies of Margaret Thatcher

Money, Ernle, *Margaret Thatcher: First Lady of the House* (Leslie Frewin, 1975)

Gardiner MP, George, *Margaret Thatcher* (William Kimber, 1975)

Lewis, Russell, *Margaret Thatcher: A Personal and Political Biography* (Routledge, 1977)

Cosgrave, Patrick, *Margaret Thatcher: A Tory and Her Party* (Hutchinson, 1978)

Murray, Patricia, *Margaret Thatcher: A Profile* (W.H. Allen, 1978)

Mayer, Allan, *Madam Prime Minister* (Newsweek Books (US), 1979)

Wapshott, Nicholas and Brock, George, *Thatcher* (Macdonald, 1983)

Lewis, Russell, *Margaret Thatcher, A Personal and Political Biography – Updated* (Routledge, 1983)

Junor, Penny, *Margaret Thatcher: Wife, Mother, Politician* (Sidgwick and Jackson, 1983)

Arnold, Bruce, *Margaret Thatcher: A Study in Power* (Hamish Hamilton, 1984)

Cosgrave, Patrick, *Thatcher: The First Term* (Bodley Head, 1985)

Harris, Kenneth, *Thatcher* (Weidenfeld and Nicolson, 1988)

Thompson, Andrew, *Margaret Thatcher: The Woman Within* (W.H. Allen, 1989)

Abse, Leo, *Margaret Daughter of Beatrice* (Jonathan Cape, 1989)

Young, Hugo, *One of Us* (Macmillan, 1989)

Ogden, Chris, *Maggie: An Intimate Portrait of a Woman in Power* (Simon and Schuster (US), 1990)

Geelhoed, Bruce, *Margaret Thatcher In Victory and Downfall* (Praeger (US), 1992)

Index